Raul Vega

Joe Queenan is a contributing writer for *Men's Health*, a columnist for *Smart Money*, and writes regularly for *The New York Times*. He recently won a Sports Emmy for his work on HBO's *Inside the NFL*. He lives in Tarrytown, New York.

Queenan Country

A RELUCTANT ANGLOPHILE'S PILGRIMAGE
TO THE MOTHER COUNTRY

JOE QUEENAN

PICADOR

HENRY HOLT AND COMPANY
NEW YORK

www.picadorusa.com

Picador® is a U.S. registered trademark and is used by Henry Holt and Company under license from Pan Books Limited.

For information on Picador Reading Group Guides, as well as ordering, please contact Picador.
Phone: 646-307-5626
Fax: 212-253-9627
E-mail: readinggroupguides@picadorusa.com

DESIGNED BY KELLY S. TOO

Library of Congress Cataloging-in-Publication Data

Queenan, Joe.
    Queenan country : a reluctant Anglophile's pilgrimage to the mother country / Joe Queenan.
        p.   cm.
    ISBN 0-312-42521-X
    EAN 978-0-312-42521-0
    1. Great Britain—Description and travel.   2. Queenan, Joe—Travel—Great Britain.   I. Title.

DA632.Q44   2004
914.104'859—dc22   2004047438

First published in the United States by Henry Holt and Company

First Picador Edition: December 2005

10 9 8 7 6 5 4 3 2 1

To the Mighty Spinners

CONTENTS

Introduction: A Passage to Indian Take-Out   1

1. No Mersey   11

2. Queen for a Day   36

3. I Left My Love in Avalon   50

4. Oh Christ, Not the Mill *and* the Floss!   69

5. First Prize: One Week in Wales   94

6. Take It to Ye Olde Limit One More Time   101

7. The Prince of Wails   127

8. 10 Things I Hate About Britain. No, Make That 20   142

9. Sweep Through the Heather   171

10. Hadrian's Wall—and Step on It!   194

11. Rule, Britannia   215

Acknowledgments   241

Queenan Country

A Passage to Indian Take-Out

While serving in the Royal Air Force during the Second World War, my wife's uncle Gordon had occasion to bomb some of the most beautiful countries in Europe. The future wing commander, just a boy at the time, had bombed the Germans, he had bombed the Italians, he had bombed the Austrians, the Hungarians, and the Romanians, and he may have bombed the French. Years later, when I first made his acquaintance in 1977, he was confined to a wheelchair in the tiny village of Charing, a stone's throw from Canterbury. He had lost his legs to gangrene after his wife died, and was living with his sister Margaret, herself a widow. Back in those days, desperate for a hobby, he would busy himself making his own Kentish wines, which he impishly compared to the finest Bordeaux. These concoctions were cheerfully horrid, but as he had been instrumental in terminating the Thousand-Year Reich 988 years ahead of schedule, I thought it my duty to force them as far down my gullet as they would go.

My wife, Francesca, whom I had met in 1974 in the quaint Philadelphia suburb of Jenkintown, never once went home to England without visiting Uncle Gordon and Aunty Margaret. On frosty nights, Margaret would stoke up the electric blankets hours in advance of our arrival. The crotchety siblings were chipper and game, and many a frosty evening we would sit in their living room camped out in front of the telly marveling at the adroit badinage of *The Two Ronnies*. As my own grandparents had died long before I was born, Margaret and Gordon were the closest things to grandparents I ever had. I adored them.

As a rule, my wife and I would stop off to see the pair on our way to France, where we would visit my wife's brother, Max, who lived near Amiens, a lackluster city with a breathtaking cathedral. The ferryboat at Dover is just a short trip down the road from Charing, meaning that we could say our good-byes at nine in the morning and be in Jules Verne's hometown by late afternoon.

"You're quite taken with the French, aren't you?" Gordon remarked one muggy afternoon as we sat watching Jimmy Connors demolish John McEnroe at Wimbledon.

"I accept them on their own terms," I replied. "They're hard to deal with, but have many fine cheeses and impressive châteaux."

"So I've been told," Gordon replied, reaching for another glass of Château de Canterbury. "Can't say I care for the French."

"But France is a beautiful country," I protested. "You have to admit that."

At this point, Gordon dropped the other shoe.

"I've never actually been there," he said. "I thought I might get across the channel one day, but now that I'm stuck in this wheelchair, I doubt that I ever will."

Charing, as noted previously, is no more than thirty miles from the White Cliffs of Dover. France itself is only twenty-two miles across the Channel. Gordon, in his capacity as a wing commander, had been all over the world, and had spent many years in this lovely region of England. But he had never actually set foot in France.

It turned out that Gordon had a number of other shocking gaps in his tourist résumé. He had been stationed in Iraq in the 1950s, but had never visited Baghdad. He had been stationed in Yorkshire without once visiting York. He had bombed Berlin, Hamburg, Toulon, Bremen, and the suburbs of Bucharest but had never seen any of them from closer than ten thousand feet. At the time, I took this to be a classic example of English insularity and good-natured xenophobia. Later, I began to have my doubts. After twenty-five years of marriage to Gordon's niece, I was beginning to think that the wing commander's eccentric travel habits were a family tradition. My wife hails from Stroud, a tiny town in the Cotswolds that is neither especially interesting nor especially attractive, but is surrounded by picture-postcard villages and hamlets that are. The mythical Cotswold Way, which stretches from Bath to Chipping Camden, passes directly above the town. Cirencester, with its well-preserved Roman ruins, is but a short jaunt up the highway, and the equally impressive Roman plumbing miracles at Bath can be reached in an hour. Stonehenge and the Vale of the White Horse are easy junkets; Wales, with Tintern Abbey and all those brooding border castles, is not an hour away. The cathedral towns of Gloucester (where Edward II is buried), Worcester (where King John is buried), and Hereford (where no one of any consequence is buried, but which has a very presentable chained library) constitute the "Three Choirs" for which the region is famous. London, Salisbury, and Stratford-on-Avon can all be reached within two hours, and the region abounds with more Chipping Nortons and Chipping Sodburys than you can shake a stick at. Planet Stroud gives off little direct light, but it is ringed by luminous constellations.

Unfortunately, over the course of our marriage, we rarely ventured out of this particular solar system. In our twenty-plus trips to Britain, we had visited Yate but had never been to York, had been to Huntly, hundreds of miles from anywhere, but had never been to Hastings, sixty miles from London. We had visited Aberdeen but had never once set foot in Edinburgh, Glasgow, or the Isle of Skye. We had spent enormous amounts of time in dreary, depressing Birmingham, which gave the world the Spencer Davis Group, but had never been to Liverpool, which gave the world the Beatles. We had been to Oxford, but not to Cambridge; had dined in Tetbury, but never once lunched in Tintagel. Our summer vacations were rigorously constricted by family visitation duties; there was never any time to hear Sir Colin Davis at the Albert Hall or Sir André Previn at Covent Garden because we were always feasting on impromptu curries with dear friends in Bow. Over that quarter century, we got to do lots of amazing things and spend lots of time with truly wonderful people, but we always did the same amazing things, and always with the same truly wonderful people.

Two thousand and two was the year I had set aside for my first trip to Italy. Like every other middle-aged American, I had been taking Italian lessons for several years, and was now primed for radiant afternoons beneath the generous Tuscan sun. At long last, I decided to set off in February, safe in the knowledge that Andrea Bocelli and his army of tin-eared Yank aficionados would be out of the country. But at the last minute, I scrapped my plans for the same reason I always scrap my plans, because, given the choice between visiting a country where I don't know anybody and revisiting a country where I seem to know everybody, I would rather go to France or England than to Greece or Italy. So, once again, Italy went on the back burner, and I booked passage for Old Blighty.

But this time, I wasn't bringing my wife along.

This time, I wanted to see Britain for myself. For decades, I'd had Francesca by my side, patiently explaining enigmatic terms like *chuffed* and *I'm blowed*, and delineating the virtues of the tea cozy. For decades, I'd been sipping cream teas with an endless procession of Aunty Margarets, Aunty Brendas, Aunty Evies, and the redoubtable Cousin Robin. Not to mention the venerable nuns at St. Rose's, where my wife had gone to school. This time, I wanted no family obligations; I wished to get a crack at the country by myself. For once, I was going to fly solo.

The narrative that follows embodies the confessions of a reluctant Anglophile. It is not a travel book per se, as travel books are dull: If the narrator is bored in rainy Portsmouth on page 231, five'll get you ten that he'll be out of sorts in damp, sunless Southampton by page 237. Though travel figures prominently in my story, much of the narrative involves the feelings, both positive and negative, that I have developed toward my wife's native land—and toward her—over the past quarter century. Ultimately I wanted this project to be a cross between a valentine and a writ of execution, an affectionate jeremiad, if you will. It is an attempt to make clear that there are things about Britain that delight me (Chelsea Pensioners, cows on the commons, Edward VII, Keith Richards), things that appall me (Chelsea football supporters, cows on canvases, Edward VIII, Cliff Richard), and things that mystify me (why anyone would listen to English morning radio, the House of Lords, the way people dress once they turn thirty, basically, the entire society). For the truth is, the Brits have always baffled me.

My dreams of an unaccompanied trip to what many Americans think of as the home country had been long in the making. But the project only began to take a definitive shape on a semitropical Fourth of July in the year 2001 when my wife suggested that the family might like a chicken tikka masala in lieu of the customary barbecue. It was this pitiless act of gastronomic cultural oppression, coupled with dread of the fearsome Christmas pudding that awaited as dessert, that ultimately inspired me to make a solitary pilgrimage to Great Britain, seeking to penetrate to the heart of Limey darkness. I decided that I would not come back from Albion until I had finally figured out what made the British tick.

This could be one long trip.

■ ■ ■

I HAVE ALWAYS BEEN RELUCTANT TO MAKE BROAD, SWEEPING statements about the "national character" of a people. On my first trip to England, in March 1976, I watched with a kind of horrified fascination as a gang of English thugs on a midnight ferry from Le Havre to Southampton terrorized the French passengers all night. The drunken goons, playing reptiles to the frogs, had sloshed across the channel to see their team pummel the French in Paris, but the French had pasted them. Now the Saxons were getting their own back, threatening to throw anyone who looked even vaguely French overboard. The French were easy to single out: The men all wore tight blue jeans and leather jackets, suggesting James Dean without the irreproducible Hoosier swagger, and the women were all quite easy on the eyes.

When I have recounted this tale over the years, British people have always sighed that such behavior was only to be expected, as soccer fans are notorious louts. But these weren't soccer fans; they were rugby fans. The enshrined mythology of the island kingdom clearly distinguishes between soccer, "a sport played by gentlemen for thugs," and rugby, "a sport played by thugs for gentlemen," so it was inconceivable to those in the know that rugby supporters, the very flower of Christian manhood, could have behaved in this way. But they had. I saw it. I was there.

In the mid-1990s, I hosted a BBC program called *Postcard from Gotham*. The producer was Hamish Mykura, a truly fabulous man who never carried even the tiniest amount of cash on or about his person. The day he hired me for the job, I was maneuvered into paying for the celebratory drinks after he blithely announced, "Oh dear; I seem to have come out without my wallet." I worked with Hamish for several years, and never saw his wallet, nor any credible evidence of its existence. A lesser man would have imputed this tightfistedness to Hamish's Scottish ethnic heritage, but in fact Mykura's parents came over from Hungary after the war. I have no idea whether Hungarians exhibit a congenital aversion to paying for anything, but it demonstrates once again that one must be very careful in drawing conclusions about the prototypical behavior of this or that ethnic group. For example, I personally do not care a great deal about money, a confession that can get you lynched in America. Of course, the main reason I don't care about money is because I have some.

All that said, it is clear that the inhabitants of Great Britain, and particularly the English, share certain common characteristics. They plan too much. They do not like to improvise. They fear that rationing may one day come back. They cannot make up their minds about the royals. They are repelled by American businessmen, but wish they could be more like them. They pack emergency sarnies, even when they are only going as far as the filling station. They are embarrassed that they lost their empire; even more embarrassed that they had it in the first place; but would secretly like to have it back, if only for the weekend, or for a few hours on Boxing Day. They are constantly apologizing, and do not seem terribly comfortable in their own skins. By contrast, even the most appalling Americans are comfortable with themselves. Americans do not mind being appalling.

The English are hard to read; their cultivated civility masks an underlying severity. After his defeat at Waterloo, Napoleon decided that it would be simply smashing to retire to a country estate in England and relax for a while, not unlike the French generals captured by Marlborough a century earlier. Foreign tyrants are always making this mistake, assuming that simply because the British are unfailingly polite they won't hang you from the highest yardarm in Her Majesty's navy. Madonna is merely the latest example of this phenomenon.

I SOJOURNED TO GREAT BRITAIN IN FEBRUARY 2002 WITH THE clear intention of making my separate peace. But when I arrived in London for my tour of the island, I could not help thinking back to that maiden voyage across the channel in March 1976. At some point in the evening, my wife got so fed up with the lager louts who were terrorizing the frightened heirs of Charlemagne that she jumped up and confronted them.

"You're the reason we lost our empire!" she declared. That stopped them dead in their tracks. It was unexpected. It was recondite. It was oracular. It was what the cowering French might call *insolite*. My wife was the first English person I'd ever met whom I actually liked; most of the Brits of my acquaintance up until that point were the maddening twits and tightwads that Britain, which has been exporting her worst for centuries, regularly foists upon unsuspecting societies. I was attracted to Francesca at least in part because she is refined and elegant, but when angered has a tendency to utter bulldoggish pronouncements of this nature.

I admired her tenacity. I envied her courage. I was highly impressed by her arch turn of phrase. I suspect that at some level, I decided to marry my wife because when you wed a woman from Britain, you secretly hoped that you might succeed in transmitting the blood of Boadicea to your children.

But Boadicea was put to the sword by the Romans for similar verbal audacity. Frankly, I'm still amazed that we got off that boat alive.

1

No Mersey

It is widely agreed, at least by everyone I know, that the British people invented the concept of ambiguity. For example, the term *British* has no precise meaning. Some people think it refers to the English, but Great Britain includes Scotland and Wales, and nobody thinks of the rugged Scots or the cranky Welsh as "Brits." The terms *Brits* and *British* are suffused with a subliminal suggestion of latent ponciness: cucumber sandwiches, sticky wickets, cream teas, tasty bickies, getting all squiffy, Noël Coward. In making this assertion, I do not mean to suggest that the British, whoever they may be, are in fact poncey, or that there is anything wrong with being poncey. But the Scots and the Welsh definitely do not fit this description. Whatever Limeys are, they are not.

Others are under the impression that the term *British* applies to denizens of the United Kingdom. But this is equally untrue, as Great Britain does not include Northern Ireland.

Even if it did, no one considers Northern Ireland's seditious Catholics British, nor do that miserable country's fractious, bellicose Protestants conjure up the image of Wimbledon Collection refinement, impeccable taste, respect for tradition, and occasional silliness that we associate with the concept of "Britishness." The Northern Irish, with their balaclava masks and machine guns, are simply not *Mikado* material.

Still other people believe that the term *Britain* applies to the original inhabitants of England, whose descendants now live in Wales. But the residents of Wales are more likely the descendants of the Celts or the Druids, and the Celts and the Druids have nothing in common with the Brits. No Brit, not even a Manchester United supporter, would have ever stormed into battle painted every color of the rainbow and naked as a prehistoric jaybird, much less dragged gigantic monoliths all the way from the mountains of Wales to Stonehenge merely to placate a vengeful, heliocentric god. Whatever they are, the Brits are not show-offs. Norman Davies goes on for pages and pages about this subject in his fascinating, controversial, but fundamentally unreadable *The Isles,* which cautions that the term *British* should be used sparingly, if at all, because it does not really mean anything.

I disagree. And apparently, so do the British people. I think the British—whoever they are—embrace the term *British* because it conveys a vivid sense of not being American or French, of remaining somehow above the fray in a venomously coarse world. Moreover, it perfectly captures the intrinsic randomness and confusion that is at the epicenter of the British character. Unlike Americans, who want everything to be cut and dried, the British people—who may or may not exist—are quite comfortable with a civilization that is a complete mess. The British people do not seem at all put off by the idea that national identity is fluid, malleable, and vague, that history is simply a vast jigsaw puzzle where many of the pieces are missing. Thus, even though a cohesive unit that can be called the British People probably does not exist, there can be no denying that they invented the concept of ambiguity, because it is obviously not the work of fiercely straightforward people like the Germans, the Russians, the Japanese, the Americans, or the French. And it is certainly not an invention of the Canadians.

Several years ago, the English historian Paul Johnson hit upon the clever idea of doubling America's heritage by declaring that the noble experiment known as the United States did not begin in 1775 at Concord and Lexington, much less in 1776 at Philadelphia, but in 1607 in Jamestown. While the approach adopted in his iconoclastic *A History of the American People* is not without methodological merit, it is just the sort of thing no sensible American academic would ever think of doing, because Americans already have enough history to keep track of, and don't need any more inventory.

But it is hardly surprising that an English historian should make the mistake of thinking that culturally deprived Americans would yearn for more history and more mythology, because this is one of Great Britain's greatest problems. It has entirely too much history. It has too many legendary historical figures. And it has too many legendary historical figures that the British people have never crystallized their true feelings toward.

The record is clear. Or, rather, let us say that the record is unclear, but the record of the record is pristine and limpid. Henry II was a truly great king who dragged Saxon Britain out of the Dark Ages, but he is mostly remembered for murdering his best friend, Thomas à Becket (see *Becket*), and for mistreating his wife, Eleanor of Aquitaine (see *The Lion in Winter*). Also, he was French. Therefore, his stature in British history is ambiguous. Edward I is widely viewed as one of the greatest English kings, yet no one thinks his treatment of William Wallace was particularly classy; having subjected him to being hanged, drawn, and quartered, did he also have to throw in the additional humiliation of ritual public castration? (This was left out of Mel Gibson's *Braveheart* because the studio wanted a PG rating and most actors view it as career-threatening to either kiss another man or be gelded on screen.) And while we're on the subject of the Scots, Bonnie Prince Charlie remains the focus of many colorful myths (see *Kidnapped*), yet most historians, and a good many Scots, regard him as an idiot.

The verdict on Henry VIII is similarly confusing. By making the fatal break with Rome in 1532, Henry VIII threw off the insatiable demands of a corrupt Catholic Church. (Five hundred years later, Boston still has not.) He also made an immense contribution to British tourism by destroying every monastery and abbey worth pillaging. No one today would make an arduous side trip to Glastonbury, which is teeming with hippies, warlocks, neo-Druids, and people looking for Merlin so they can buy some drugs off him, or Tintern Abbey, a rambling wreck that is all the way out in the middle of nowhere, merely to see a standing house of worship. But for some reason ancient ruins exert an almost hypnotic power over the hoi polloi.

Yet Henry VIII is remembered as a deranged porker who murdered two of his wives, one of whom had six fingers and three breasts, which in and of themselves would have persuaded most red-blooded males to go easy on her. It was quite a family: Anne Boleyn, winner of the mammarian trifecta, was sent to the scaffold by her husband for not producing a male heir—at least not one that would have resembled him, as she clearly got around. Yet Anne gave birth to the greatest potentate of them all. Ironically, Elizabeth Regina herself was nearly executed by her bloodthirsty half sister Mary, daughter of Catherine of Aragon, and, perhaps in revenge for this slight, wrote the death warrant for her much-admired cousin, the flashy but addled Mary Queen of Scots, whose own son James I signed off on her beheading, only to have *his* own son, Charles I, dealt the exact same fate by Oliver Cromwell.

Actually, none of this is particularly ironic.

Mary, Queen of Scots is marinated in so much romance that it is difficult to draw a bead on her. To the great unwashed, she has earned her niche in the Pantheon of the Immortals as a vaunted heroine, a feminist role model and a tragic figure, a Boadicea in ermine, pitied because she was executed simply for being Catholic. But she was also a scheming, traitorous tart who married the man who murdered her first husband. And she went bald early. (This is probably why she is viewed as a feminist role model.)

This schizoid mind-set is very different from the way Americans treat their legends. Basically, all sensible Americans regard Washington, Lincoln, and Teddy Roosevelt as saintly figures, and opinion is similarly undivided on Sitting Bull, Robert E. Lee, and Calamity Jane. FDR was such an important historical figure that not even Republicans dare deny his greatness. And despite occasional revisionist efforts to demean the character of both Thomas Jefferson and Woodrow Wilson, these are the spurious efforts of a few mean-spirited academics, the sort Dickens derided as "the insects of the moment," and no one takes them very seriously. The American people like their history to be black and white, fixed for time immemorial. Plenty of people living in Britain today honestly believe that Henry VII, not Richard III, killed the little princes. Others do not. But everybody in the United States knows that Richard Nixon, our own evil little hunchback, was capable of any crime, no matter how monstrous. Even people who voted for Nixon hated him; he rarely smiled and when he did it frightened even Republican children. In saying this, I mean no offense to American hunchbacks, few of whom are explicitly evil, and most of whom are probably Democrats, as the Republicans cut off benefits to hunchbacks decades ago.

A BRIEF VISIT TO WESTMINSTER PROVIDES US WITH A VIVID example of the ambiguity, indecisiveness, and general confusion that animate British history. Outside the Houses of Parliament stand two visually arresting monuments: a statue of Oliver Cromwell, leaning on his mighty sword, and an equestrian statue of Richard the Lion-Hearted. Not far away stands a massive statue of Winston Churchill. These three titans are fixtures both of British history and of British mythology, yet in all three cases the British people display feelings toward them that are decidedly mixed.

Richard I is the romantic crusader, champion of the common people, and boon companion of Robin Hood, who is forever linked with his malignant younger brother, the scheming King John, and his nefarious henchman, the Sheriff of Nottingham (see *Costner, Kevin*). A snappy dresser who once dined with Saladin, the Yasser Arafat of his time, Richard was a fearless warrior who died when felled by an archer after wandering too close to the walls of Chaluz in order to better taunt his besieged adversaries. Owing to his jaunty image and unparalleled sense of occasion, Richard the Lion-Hearted is rivaled only by Camelot's King Arthur (see *Excalibur*) for sheer mythological power, and possesses the additional advantage of having actually existed.

But Richard I was an irresponsible king who bankrupted his kingdom through his inept campaigns and the huge ransom that had to be paid for his release when he was imprisoned by scheming Teutons. During his entire ten-year reign, he spent only six months in England, returning just long enough to raise more cash so that he could go back to his foolish gallivanting on the continent. In this sense, he resembles Fergie, another gluttonous, improvident royal who spends a great deal of time overseas, occasionally returning home to raise more cash through modern scutage when the revenues from Weight Watchers International have dried up.

These are not the only charges that can be leveled against Richard the Lion-Hearted. His campaigns in the Holy Land were largely unsuccessful. His sexual predilections were highly suspect. It was his brother, not he, who signed the

Magna Carta, the document that laid the foundation for the Anglo-American democratic system, the greatest innovation in all of history. Worst of all, he was French.

Oliver Cromwell's place in the heart of the British people is even more tenuous. By deposing and executing the profligate Charles I, he sounded the death knell for the divine right of kings and can arguably be called the father of the English Republic. Well, perhaps more like the stepfather. But he was a morose, vindictive butcher, and it was unpleasant to live in Britain while he was alive. It was even less fun to live in Ireland, where Cromwell carried on a near genocidal war of terror, and is hated to this day. Centuries after his death, one still encounters Irish-Americans who use the term "May the Curse of Cromwell be upon you," though most of them are frat boys at McSorley's who grew up in suburban Ohio. Though not French, Cromwell ended his public career by having his festering corpse exhumed, dismembered, beheaded, and tossed onto a dung heap, which is basically the same thing. Though rumors persist that his skull, which hung on a spike for twenty years, can be seen in a museum somewhere in East Anglia, no one knows for sure what happened to the rest of his body. Quick: Name another society that would erect a statue outside the headquarters of its principal legislative body memorializing a tyrant whose corpse was thrown onto a dung heap. Take lots of time with your answer.

Winston Churchill is another majestic figure whose overall record generates considerable dispute. Though no one, not even Christopher Hitchens, denies that he single-handedly saved Western Civilization from the marauding Hun, he was voted out of office before the war was over because working-class people viewed him as a reactionary. The implacable enemy of social progress, a legendary strike breaker, and the architect of the Allied disaster at Gallipoli, the opportunistic, self-promoting Churchill would have died forgotten and unloved had Adolf Hitler not presented him with a golden opportunity to rescue Western Civilization from the marauding Hun. Thus, even though he is universally admired—except by Christopher Hitchens—for compelling the maruading Hun to stop marauding, Churchill's legacy is somewhat mixed.

TO THE OUTSIDER, IT IS VERY DIFFICULT TO UNDERSTAND British history, because the British people themselves do not understand it. I have lost track of the number of evenings I have lain awake in a mildewy Cotswold attic baying at the moon, disconsolate because I could not figure out whose idea it was to kill Lady Jane Grey, why Lady Guinevere bedded down with an unreliable mercenary, or why Scottish kings named James kept accepting invitations to their sworn enemies' foreboding castles after what happened to William Wallace when he showed up for a similar rendezvous. And, for the life of me, I have no idea what precipitated the War of the Roses. It does not help that York was a stronghold of the House of Lancaster, not the House of York. Nor does it help that the city of York, despite its traditional leanings toward the House of Lancaster, mourned the passing of the Yorkist Richard III, even though he was from the south, and technically the duke of Gloucester, the largest city in Britain without a professional football team, though it does hold the British record for indoor mass murders. It is as if Ulysses S. Grant hailed from

Virginia and Jeb Stuart from rural Maine. It is simply impossible to keep things straight.

Inevitably, this brings us to the true focal point of this chapter, a legendary figure who straddles English society like a colossus and who, like so many other colossi of the nation's richly perplexing history, is both loved and hated. Saint and sinner, genius and cretin, hero and traitor, no figure in recent British history elicits such conflicting emotions as this man. A tyro who brought the British people as much joy as Charles II, yet who betrayed them as wantonly as Guy Fawkes; an enigma who combined the radiant charm of Elizabeth I with the perverse dowdiness of Elizabeth II; a youth who shone with the brilliance of Henry V at Agincourt, before succumbing to the senescent foolishness of a Henry VI anywhere, he is a historical anomaly, the one individual who embodies all the disparate strands of love and hate that typify the British people.

I am speaking, of course, of Paul McCartney.

The saga of Paul McCartney is too well known to repeat. Nevertheless, I shall repeat it here, because this is what sagas are for. McCartney was a working-class lad from grim, despondent Liverpool who formed a group called the Beatles, which took the world by storm in 1964, just shortly after John F. Kennedy's death, events that are probably not unrelated. For the next three or four years, the entire planet had a song in its heart and a bounce in its step due to the ministrations of the Fab Four and the carefree era they inspired. But then the world turned evil and personal antipathies involving dueling consorts caused the band to fall apart. Popular mythology holds that McCartney went on to make an uninterrupted series of revoltingly sappy records, both with Wings and as a solo performer, while Lennon took the high road and made a number of very entertaining, very adventurous, somewhat less commercially successful LPs.

But this is a deliberate falsification of the historical record. Not all of McCartney's solo music is awful; he made a very fine throwback record (*Run Devil Run*) in 1999, and an equally interesting record (*CHOBA B CCCP: The Russian Album*) in 1987. While it's true that Wings studio LPs are generally quite flatulent, there are a number of solid tracks on the band's live record *Wings over America*, and a few snappy tunes like "Veronica" and "The World Tonight" on subsequent McCartney releases. I am not arguing that McCartney's post-sixties work even vaguely compares to his collaborations with his fellow Beatles; I am merely saying that it is nowhere near as bad as the critics maintain.

By contrast, John Lennon's musical legacy is ludicrously overrated. Though it was not apparent at the time, because Lennon's charismatic personality, cunning wordplay, and overall style served as diversionary tactics to shield his primitive, self-indulgent music from evenhanded criticism, Lennon's solo records generally stink, and the ones he made with Yoko Ono are by this late date virtually unlistenable. No one ever plays "Instant Karma," "Power to the People," or "Woman Is the Nigger of the World" these days; their time has come and gone. True, Lennon recorded a handful of good songs like "Jealous Guy" and "Give Peace a Chance," but McCartney recorded equally worthy songs like "Helen Wheels" and "Maybe I'm Amazed." As for the other Beatles, George Harrison never improved on his youthful *All Things*

Must Pass; his later records were languid, dull, excessively mystical, and sometimes foolish. His only mature work of any consequence is the material he recorded with the Traveling Wilburys, when he received lots of help from Tom Petty, Roy Orbison, Bob Dylan, and the fugitive from ELO. Finally, when was the last time anyone cued up a Ringo Starr platter on the turntable? By contrast, Paul has made several records in living memory that are loud, vibrant, and entertaining. To an extent.

It is true that Paul has a smarmy, unctuous side, that he has gradually evolved into a Zen master of feigned humility. He both looks and sounds like butter would not melt in his mouth, an unforgivable trait in a rock star living in a post-Jagger, post-Morrison, post-Cobain era. Too desperate to please, he often acts as if he does not fully believe he deserves his fame. He is the kind of person it is easy to hate, if only because he wrote the lyrics to "Michelle." Yet personally, I have always resented the duplicity of the British people in blaming him for songs like "Michelle." For in asserting that "Michelle" and "ma belle" are words that go "très bien" together, McCartney was merely crystallizing the sentiments of his emotionally flabby nation. The English speak French worse than the French speak English, something that is almost impossible to do. In a single song Paul captured the intrinsic vulgarity of the British middle classes, who are never more crude than when they are trying to be sophisticated. There is a direct line from "Michelle" to Rod Stewart's *Great American Songbook* to the Grimethorpe Colliery UK Coal Band's staggeringly pretentious concert arrangements of such imperishable classics as "Mambo Caliente" and

"Evergreen" (see *Brassed Off* and *A Star Is Born*). But if it is Paul's crime for writing "Michelle," whose crime is it for listening?

In my mind, Paul McCartney is merely the latest in a long line of great British historical figures—the British Lions—who started out being beloved by the common people, only to earn their undying enmity as they grew older together. Though he is easy to despise and has much to answer for, it cannot be denied that he brought much joy into the world. And so it was that I sojourned to Liverpool, with a deep-seated desire to get back to where I once belonged. Just as surely as I needed to gaze at the Sistine Chapel, kiss the Blarney Stone, and watch the Philadelphia Eagles hoist the Super Bowl trophy before finally meeting my maker, I needed to visit Paul's house as a way of saying "thanks."

THE SECRET TO EFFECTIVE TOURISM IS TO QUICKLY DISPOSE of the cultural compulsories in the morning, so you can spend the rest of the day doing the things that really interest you (ride on the London Eye, watch Arsenal ream Chelsea, consort with a Scandinavian Natural Blond Transsexual Mistress whose rates are actually quite reasonable). Arriving in Liverpool very early in the day, I whipped through the city's two modern cathedrals. The Catholic edifice, built in the 1960s, is a towering spaceship filled with vaulting stained-glass windows that permit divine light to shine down on the edified congregation. Festive, gay, and not at all solemn, it stands in marked contrast to the dowdy city it towers above. A paean to Liverpool's teeming masses of proud Irish immigrants, it looks like something you would see in San Francisco, if San Francisco had any teeming immigrant masses it was proud of. No architecture buff, I have no way of knowing whether it is beautiful or merely silly, but one thing is certain: Were Oliver Cromwell alive today, he would gut it in five minutes flat.

The gloomy, fortresslike Protestant cathedral was another matter entirely. Physically the most massive structure in Anglican Britain, it pays homage to a dour, cheerless god the English people stopped believing in back in the eighteenth century when they started worshipping Mammon. It reminded me of the Cathedral of St. John the Divine in upper Manhattan, a medieval superstructure entirely lacking the philosophical underpinnings of the Renaissance. In Liverpool, it was as if the congregation had run out of money to pay Frank Gehry to do something swoopy and funky, and instead furnished the architect with floor plans left over from the ninth century. Nevertheless, I browbeat an American tourist into taking off his baseball cap as he approached the altar, because I believe that one should always show respect in houses of worship, even if one does not believe in the deities that are venerated there. I might add that I have always had problems with the Anglican god worshipped by contemporary Brits; he seems more like a respected barrister than a hard-core fire-and-brimstone divinity. Of course, I was brought up as a soldier in the Army of Christ.

As is so often the case with modern churches, the cathedral was filled with very bad art, in this case large paintings by one Adrian Wiszniewski. One canvas, which fuses the worst of Fernand Léger with the even worse of Roy Lichtenstein,

depicted a naked young slackeress being offered a chalice by
a woman who may have been Mary Magdalene. The young
woman's sexual organs were clearly visible. I could not recall
which part of the Bible this episode was from; the Douay-
Rheims version favored by Irish Catholics like me tends not
to go in much for exposed genitals. Once again, the Anglicans
seemed to be going off in an entirely new direction. True, religious iconography had been heading straight downhill since
the late Renaissance, but this objet d'art was particularly trou-
bling. It did not make me stop believing in God. But it gave
me second thoughts about art.

The theological prelims out of the way, I ambled down to
the harbor and took the ferry cross the Mersey. The chatty
guide filled us in on Liverpool's rich history as a port, ship-
building hub, Celtic breeding center, and point of embarka-
tion for innumerable emigrants to the New World. He
directed our attention to numerous famous buildings, many
pertaining to the cotton trade. Or was it flax? He conceded
that Liverpool, pummeled by the Luftwaffe, had fallen on
hard times after the war, but was now a city on the rebound,
having been the recipient of considerable investment capital
from the European Union. I was very happy for Liverpool, as
it clearly possessed a gritty charm and deserved a helping
hand.

Back on terra firma, homework out of the way, I got down
to cases, reporting to the ticket office operated by an organi-
zation called the Magical Mystery Tour. (Similar tour groups
may exist for the Stone Roses in Manchester or Wham! in
London, but I have no way of knowing.) Unfortunately, I was
too late. I was told in no uncertain terms that I had missed the

last bus to the neighborhood where the Beatles had grown up. The woman at the disinformation desk warned me that it was pointless to proceed by taxi, as my destination was miles and miles away, and the ride would cost me a fortune. Moreover, tourists were expressly forbidden to visit the district, because the neighbors disliked them intensely.

None of this was true.

Hailing a cab at the Liverpool train station, I asked the ruddy-faced driver if I could visit the Beatles' homes and get back in time for the 4:45 train to London, where I had an important appointment with someone whose name I now forget. The driver, a cheerful, garrulous sort whom we shall refer to as Big Jim, said that this was indeed possible, as John's house was only twelve minutes away.

"You're in luck today," Big Jim chuckled, as we roared past the legendary Cavern Club and veered out toward the quaint, not-at-all-depressing community where John had grown up. "John Lennon was best man at my wedding."

I was astounded, unable to believe my good fortune. What were the odds of bumping into a complete stranger who could lay claim to being an intimate of the Fab Four? Even in the city of their fab birth. But Big Jim's personal involvement in the evolution and dissemination of the Mersey Beat most assuredly did not stop there. A native of Liverpool, he had been a member of a well-respected trio called the Big Three, once managed by the elusive, sphinxlike Brian Epstein. Epstein, an entertainment industry dynamo, went on to guide the Beatles to unimaginable international fame before taking his own life in 1967. Though the Big Three had long

receded into the mists of time, to this very day Big Jim continued to keep their memory alive.

"What was John like?" I inquired, as we rocketed off into
semisuburban Liverpool.

"He was not the type to tolerate fools gladly," Big Jim
informed me. "If he didn't like you, he didn't mind letting you
know. And he had a temper. Oh, yes. One night, after he'd
had a row with Cynthia [Lennon's first wife and mother of
Julian], I told him, 'John, if you ever lay a hand on Cynthia
again, you and I are going outside.'"

I was impressed. And jealous. Though I had appeared on
the late-night American television show *Politically Incorrect*
with Graham Nash and the lead singers from both Bad Religion and Asleep at the Wheel, and had once hobnobbed with
Ian Anderson of Jethro Tull at a concert in Tarrytown, New
York, the closest I had ever gotten to "going outside" with a
legitimate rock star was when I briefly stared daggers at the
lead guitarist from Anthrax. Pathetic. Big Jim, on the other
hand, had been present at the creation. What a treasure
trove of information he proved to be! Photographing me outside the run-down children's home called Strawberry Fields,
Big Jim explained that the sign had once been stolen by local
ne'er-do-wells. This I had not known. We then proceeded to
the two houses John once called home, then the pub that
served as the cover for Ringo's first solo album, then George's
house, then Ringo's aunt's house, and finally Penny Lane
itself. I felt like Balboa, sighting the mighty Pacific for the
first time.

Along the way, Big Jim brought me up to speed on the

Beatles' status vis-à-vis the local populace. John, of course, was viewed as a god, even though by the time he died in 1980, he had been dead to Liverpool for almost two decades. George, though he had spent most of his later years on distant shores, had contributed a good deal of money to fixing up a famous Liverpudlian architectural crown jewel that had fallen into disrepair. Ringo was known to regularly nip back into the city and visit friends and relatives. But when I asked to see Paul's house, where I planned to kiss the doorstep or smooch the door knocker or pay some other form of grudging, long-overdue homage to the much-maligned cofounder of the band, to whom I owed so much, whatever his post-Beatles failings, Big Jim refused.

"I never cared for Paul," he said. "He's got a big head."

Though I would have dearly loved to at least catch a glimpse of Paul's ancestral abode, Big Jim would not hear of it. Pointing out that time was getting on, he sped back to the train station, where I alighted just in time to catch the 4:45 back to London. As we shook hands, I planted a wrinkled fiver in his palm. It was not a huge tip, but Big Jim did not seem like a huge tip kind of guy. We had enjoyed each other's company. We had shared a few Hogarthian guffaws. We had chatted, however briefly, about such bands as Cool Teddy and the Cruisers, Ian and the Zodiacs, and Gerry and the Pacemakers. Though our liaison was short, it was fraught with the kind of powerful emotion that has always defined the special relationship the English share with their scamplike American cousins. I told Jim that he had made the day one of the most memorable in my life. He gave me his business card and insisted I call the next time I was in Liverpool. Then we parted.

MY AFTERNOON WITH BIG JIM LEFT ME FEELING CHUFFED AS a squiffy cart pony. But soon thereafter, back in London, I was dealt a cruel reverse. I was recounting my awfully big adventure with a man who had invited John Lennon to be his best man, and who was apparently one of the pivotal figures in the whole Liverpool pop-combo sixties scene, to my friends, a young couple named Ben and Teri. Teri, a native of Indiana and a very fine musician in her own right, was impressed. But Ben, no gullible Hoosier he, was not.

"What's his name?" he asked, dubiously.

I told him.

"There was never anyone in the Big Three by that name," he grimly informed me. Oh my godfathers, I had wandered into the deepest cavern in the dankest bowels of the daunting realm of rock arcana! Ben, born in 1967, was fiendishly devoted to the music of the early 1960s, before satanic entities like Yes, Asia, King Crimson, and Emerson, Lake & Palmer went and ruined everything. He adored the Rolling Stones and the Kinks but had a special affection for obscure outfits like the Anteeks, Just4Men, and the Birds (Ronnie Wood's first outfit, and no relation to the Byrds). And while he admired the early Beatles, he stopped listening with any great enthusiasm after *Revolver,* when they started to get arty. He made regular pilgrimages to music conventions in dire locales like Allentown, Austin, and Dallas, armed with a tiny portable record player to check out the merchandise. He loved one-hit wonders, but positively worshipped no-hit wonders. He owned impossible-to-find LPs by unknown mid-sixties Pennsylvania garage bands like the Snaps, the Bats, and the Centuries. (Alas, alack, my own mid-sixties Pennsylvania garage bands, the Phase Shift Network and Baby's Death, had never committed our work to acetate.) He believed that pop music had achieved its apotheosis in the sixties, when bands churned out a steady barrage of two-minute singles, none contaminated by sitars or synthesizers. He had forgotten more about sixties pop music than anyone else ever knew. In short, I was staying in a flat with the one person in the United Kingdom who could immediately disabuse me of the notion that my cabbie had been a member of the Big Three. Ben was, in fact, on a first-name basis with the members of the Big Three: Brian Griffiths, Johnny Gustafson, and Johnny Hutchinson. And although the dimly remembered combo's lineup later included Bill Russley, Paddy Chambers, and Paul Pilnick, there was never anyone in the band matching my cabbie's description.

Ben was equally suspicious of the notion that my Liverpool-based cabdriver could possibly have been wed on Boxing Day 1964 with John Lennon in attendance. Padding over to his groaning bookshelves, he produced two almanacs that meticulously detailed the Beatles' daily activities from the moment they became famous to the moment they disbanded. (No such documentation exists for the diurnal adventures of REM, whose lead singer once dismissed the Fab Four's work as "elevator music.") On Boxing Day 1964, the Beatles were performing at the Hammersmith Odeon.

These astonishing revelations left me deeply troubled. I slept poorly that night, afflicted with self-doubt. Yesterday, as I saw it, all my troubles seemed so far away. But now I knew that they were here to stay. As a topflight journalist, I felt snookered, humiliated. I had come back from Liverpool bursting with enthusiasm because I had spent such a wonderful afternoon being chaperoned around one of pop music's two most myth-drenched proving grounds by a man who claimed to have been right there when the volcano erupted. Now I was told that my guide was a fake. And perhaps not merely him. Perhaps this was all part and parcel of a vast municipal scam. Ben wondered what would have happened had I climbed into another taxi at the Liverpool train station. Perhaps the second cabdriver would have tried to pass himself off as Ringo's brother-in-law. Perhaps the third cabbie would have claimed to have been the original bassist from Gerry and the Pacemakers. Perhaps the fourth would have assured me that he had once worked as a roadie for Slade. No, they were from Wolverhampton, seventy miles to the south. Still, the point was well taken. Big Jim had played on my heartstrings like a cheap piano. Or was it a cheap suit? Either way, the verdict was in. I was a typical American tourist with more money than brains, a shill, a gull, a stoolie, and a rube who had been hornswoggled by a canny Liverpudlian. I had fallen for the oldest trick in the book: the Big Three Gambit. I had been led down the garden path. I'd had the wool pulled over my eyes. I had been taken for a ride.

I *was* the Walrus.

But one thing about this theory bothered me. Sizing me up as an easy mark, Big Jim had identified himself as a protégé of

Brian Epstein and a ranking member of the Big Three. But Big Jim had no way of knowing that I would return to a London apartment owned by the only person I knew—perhaps the only person anybody knew—who could demolish this monstrous edifice of deceit. Let's face it, the history of the Big Three was hardly common knowledge. And what were the odds that an American tourist would make a deliberate effort to unearth his deception?

The point of it was, Big Jim could have told me a much bigger whopper about his musical background with virtually no fear that his tapestry of lies would come unwound. Yet he had not. He had not claimed to be a member of the Animals. He had not claimed to be a drinking buddy of Eric Clapton's. He made no attempt to masquerade as Stevie Winwood's cousin, Johnny Rotten's uncle, Elton John's florist. His deception, by the standards of modern popular musical deceit, had been modest indeed.

I once read a story in the *Los Angeles Times* about a mysterious homeless man who lived in a cardboard box under the Santa Monica Freeway. Everyone in the neighborhood referred to him as the Champ. An enterprising reporter had dedicated himself to researching the man's identity, reaching the preliminary conclusion that he was Bob Satterfield, a top contender for the heavyweight crown back in the early sixties. A ferocious puncher, Satterfield himself could not take a punch, and had been knocked out by Floyd Patterson, also renowned for his glass jaw. Seemingly, the peripatetic pugilist had willfully created the impression that he was Satterfield, now reduced to his impecunious fate. But upon further investigation, the reporter discovered that the bag person was not

in fact Satterfield, but another top contender who had himself been dispatched by Satterfield. Admittedly, it was strange
to pretend to be the person who had stretched you out on the
canvas. But what was the harm in that? It wasn't as if he were
telling lies to advance his career as a hobo.

This story was much in my thoughts as I reflected on the
Legend of Faux Jim. For whatever the reason, my cabbie had
invented a plausible personal mythology that stopped just
inches short of reality. I did not have it in me to begrudge him
this. Moreover, Jim's deviousness did not negate the wonderful experience we had shared. I had spent a delightful hour
cruising around Liverpool. Jim's banter had cheered me
greatly. He had not tried to shake me down for a huge tip; he
seemed more than pleased with the measly five quid I gave
him. True, there was a part of me that wanted to phone him
up and grill him on the history of the Big Three, and deci-
sively torpedo his fabrications. But I had no heart for it. If Big
Jim honestly believed that he had once been a member of the
Big Three, it was neither my right nor my duty to sabotage his
delusions.

At the end of the day, to use a piddling banality immortal-
ized by Madonna Ciccone, this unusual experience prompted
me to reflect on both the vanity of human wishes and the
absurdity of the human condition. One hundred years from
now, people will still be making pilgrimages to Beethoven's
house in Bonn and Mozart's home in Salzburg. But one hundred years from now, unless I miss my guess, no one will be
going to Liverpool to participate in any Magical Mystery Tour.
Pop music has no staying power; as an art form it is purely
generational, and as the years drift by, even the greatest are

forgotten. In a hundred years, perhaps even fifty, the Beatles' music will seem as quaint, rickety, and outmoded as Rudy Vallee's. People will visit Liverpool to see the famous docks and the anachronistic cathedrals, but no one will be interested in John, Paul, George, and Ringo. Liverpool, once great, will go back to being what it was before the Beatles put it back on the map: a poor, remote municipality whose time has passed. This is not an indictment; it is a fact.

But there will always be a place in my heart for the great city of Liverpool. However it came about, I spent one of the happiest days in my life there. And Big Jim was the reason. Whatever the truth about his musical career, his heart was in the right place. He took me to Penny Lane. He photographed me outside Ringo's aunt's house. He showed me where George Harrison grew up. He explained the strange provenance of the song title "Strawberry Fields," a locale as sacred as the Vatican to those who grew up in the sixties. And, in refusing to take me to Paul McCartney's house, he helped to crystallize my feelings about the singer. Like Oliver Cromwell, Henry VIII, Richard II, and Macbeth, Paul had started life well but ended it badly. A supernova in his youth, a hero to his people, he had, with the passage of time, succumbed to the base instincts that had perhaps always lurked in his bosom, like a smarmy adder in a basket of chrysanthemums. The good that had come from "I Saw Her Standing There" and "Please Please Me" had been supplanted by the evil of "Ebony and Ivory" and "Silly Love Songs." Paul could be forgiven for the obstreperous hokiness of "My Love" and "Uncle Albert" ("Hands Across the Water") but he could never be absolved of the harm he had wrought with "Yesterday" and "Michelle." Much less Wings. The long and winding road had not led me to his door, for Big Jim had refused to take me there. When I found myself in times of trouble, Mother Mary had not come to me, but Big Jim had. I had gone to Liverpool, my heart bubbling with treacle, determined to write a spirited defense of Paul McCartney. Big Jim, by a simple act of refusing to make a right turn, had saved me from abject disgrace. Big Jim, in my view, taken for what it is worth, such as it is, you will *always* be the man who had John Lennon stand by your side on your wedding day. You will *always* be the scrapper who threatened to punch out John's lights if he ever laid hands on Cynthia again. And yes, you will *always* be a member of the Big Three.

Whoever the hell the Big Three are.

2

Queen for a Day

The great cities of the world are best thought of in terms of flora and fauna. San Francisco is a hyacinth, Rio de Janeiro a bromeliad, Cairo a flowering cactus, Detroit a burning bush. London, by contrast, most closely resembles a Venus flytrap. Intoxicated by its shimmering exterior, tourists the world over are helplessly drawn to this imperial city, a bustling, history-drenched metropolis that was old when Paris was young. With its dazzling roster of reassuringly familiar delights—Big Ben, Beefeaters, bobbies, Buckingham Palace—London at first glance appears hospitable, refreshing, perhaps even wholesome. It looks like a city you can have fun in, a city that will give you a fighting chance, a city that won't hit you on the head and leave you for dead.

This is precisely how the trap gets sprung. From a distance, London seems completely *normal*, a very big, very exciting city that happens to be filled with millions of ordinary people—just like you! With its combination of coziness, tradition, charm, and seeming accessibility, London lures its unsuspecting prey to its demise. The guileless tourist arrives with his heart in his mouth and his cash in his hand, honestly believing that London is a city he can handle, a city he can master, a city he can tame. Then he ventures out into the streets and London swallows him whole.

Sheer size has much to do with this. The greatest mistake the traveler makes in taking a crack at London is in assuming that the city is somehow manageable. It is not. It is physically massive and bristling with literally hundreds of attractions the serious tourist will feel morally obligated to investigate at close hand. Achieving these tasks cannot be accomplished in a week or a month; it is the work of a lifetime. Some of these activities are expensive, many involve waiting in line for long periods of time. All of them impose excessive demands on the nervous system and the spinal cord. Several require far-flung trips on public transportation, most specifically the daunting tube, a maze of ostensibly interconnected labyrinths enabling travelers to stagger three-quarters of a mile by foot just so they can ride three hundred yards up Tottenham Court Road.

No one should attempt to visit London without first undergoing a complete physical; the city is most assuredly not recommended for small children, who will inevitably whine about the traffic, the hotel water pressure, the odor of cilantro that dominates entire neighborhoods, and the overly ambitious itinerary their parents have devised. If you have not visited London by the age of sixty-five, try Brussels instead: Your feet won't be able to take it. Or, if you're really determined to check London off your dream itinerary, gamble that the

Hindus are right about reincarnation, seal up the windows and doors, turn on the gas jets, and in your next karmic manifestation don't wait so long to visit England, you knucklehead.

Also, bring thick socks.

Whenever I have visited London I have always engaged in a certain amount of high-minded tourism, but have taken pains to do so in stages: the Albert Hall, Trafalgar Square, the Tate Britain, and Regent's Park Zoo on one trip; Westminster Abbey, St. Paul's Cathedral, Speaker's Corner, and the Greenwich Observatory the next. I ease my foot off the accelerator; I know I will be passing through these parts again. But most people do not pace themselves; they are desperate to "do" London once and get it out of the way, so that they can "do" Honolulu or Muscle Shoals next trip. Whenever I visit London, I am smitten by an unexpected, utterly uncharacteristic compassion for the teeming masses huddled in the rain outside Buckingham Palace, the Tower of London, the Hard Rock Cafe; they seem to be reporting for work, performing a duty, putting in overtime, punching the clock. Ultimately, I have come to view the London experience as a tourist's Golgotha: exciting if you are a spectator, painful if you are a participant.

Unlike Barcelona or Quebec, whose cultural and historical high points can be polished off in a few days, London subjects tourists to unrelenting torment, constantly reminding them how little they have accomplished, how much remains to be seen. As a result, the first-time visitor to London comes away with precious little sense of accomplishment; he has managed to glimpse the crown jewels, videotape the kids in front of Mary, Queen of Scot's tomb in Westminster Abbey, examine

Winston Churchill's Finest Hour lodgings at the War Cabinet Rooms, and take a boat ride on the Thames, but never got a chance to scale Primrose Hill, ride on the London Eye, attend the ballet at Covent Garden, or visit the Old Curiosity Shop, much less watch Tim Henman duke it out with Greg Rusedski at Wimbledon. (Left-leaning fellow travelers might also toss in a visit to Karl Marx's tomb in Highgate.)

Due to time constraints and the sheer immensity of the city, the tourist returns home feeling shortchanged. He has bagged the National Gallery, Fortnum & Mason, Notting Hill, Brick Lane, the Sherlock Holmes Museum, and the Church of St. Martin-in-the-Fields, but secretly laments that the really big game—the Houses of Parliament, Magna Carta, the Tower of London, Harrods, the Elgin Marbles, Wellington's Tomb, the Princess Di Memorial Walk—somehow managed to elude him. The tourist always reproaches himself for only booking a weekend trip when a full seven days was necessary, for only staying a fortnight when a summer was required to do the city justice. But no matter how long you stay in London, London will wear you down and wear you out. London is intractable, insuperable, inexhaustible; the tourist is hapless, cowed, puny, and ultimately penniless. When the exchange rate is weak, London can bankrupt even the most well-heeled American in a matter of hours.

Over the years, I have taken in most of the tourist destinations for which this great city is famous. Some—St. Paul's, the British Museum, the National Gallery, Westminster Abbey, Hyde Park—I make a point of visiting each time I set foot on these shores. Others I revisit once every quarter century. Some I avoid like the plague. But one must be careful not to overlook the small pleasures. The Houses of Parliament are fine and dandy, but the moment you really feel transported to another time and place is when you find yourself relaxing in an East End pub called the Widow's Son, where the windows are filled with buns set out every year since the Napoleonic Wars in expectation of the son's return, and where all the patrons look like they work for the Krays. Piccadilly is always a thrill, but the moment you really feel the hairs standing up on your neck is when you are munching a bacon butty at the Tea Hut on Blackheath amid a phalanx of truck drivers who have driven miles out of their way to sample the eighty-year-old establishment's legendary Animal Burger. And I sometimes think that if I hadn't had the chance to lunch at the Eel & Pie Shop in Peckham, there was really no point in being born.

There are many, many Londons that tourists know nothing about, and wouldn't enjoy if they did. These include the grotty north, the prim west, the proletarian east, and the other-worldly Canary Wharf, a strange, futuristic complex built by strange, futuristic Canadians. Also worthy of mention is the mysterious no-man's-land south of the river. On my solitary trip of a lifetime to England, I set aside plenty of time to study South London in great detail, visiting Brixton, Clapham Common, and Peckham, and was pleased by what I saw. I hiked through Battersea Park, strolled around Wimbledon, spent a few hours in and around Elephant & Castle. I listened in rapt pleasure as a choir of black schoolgirls sang "Jerusalem" in Southwark Cathedral, renowned as the church where enemies of the king could briefly seek sanctuary during the Middle Ages. For too long I had slighted this much-maligned district, which lies far off the beaten tourist track. I immediately made a vow that in the future, all of my trips to this remarkable city would take me to this newfound corner of the metropolis, even though it is home to several million people everyone else looks down on, and is essentially the English equivalent of Staten Island.

Until my midlife trek to Britain I had always given the West End a wide berth. I'd lost count of the number of times I had shunned the opportunity to attend the long-running *Stones in His Pockets*, a saccharine play lionizing daft but lovable Celtic rubes. Similarly, I had never once been tempted to take a peek at *No Sex Please, We're British,* a staple of the West End theater circuit for many, many years, which friends assured me was even worse than it sounded. Also, given that the comedy was being staged in a tawdry district known hither and yon for its deviant sex industry, the very premise made no sense, unless one assumed that only foreign tourists were deviant. For whatever reason, tourists seem genetically attracted to unseemly districts where they are likely to get pickpocketed, garrotted, swindled, or indifferently serviced by precociously geriatric hookers who rarely resemble the lascivious models whose photos adorn every phone box in central London. The theater district adjoining Leicester Square more than fit this profile.

My failure to attend performances of *Stones in His Pockets* or *No Sex Please, We're British* constituted an admittedly shocking gap in my résumé as a cultural critic and self-appointed arbiter of bad taste. For decades, I had been aware of London's stature as a theatrical mecca for philistines, yet I had always stayed far away from the West End. This was inexcusable, given the district's position as a cultural early warning system; we all know that very bad, very evil things that originate in London will eventually reemerge as revered institutions in New York, Chicago, and San Francisco. *Les Miz* started here. *Phantom* started here. *Riverdance* erupted here. It is a remarkable irony that many of the best shows in London— *Chicago, Oklahoma!*—and even such harmless diversions as *The Lion King* and *Beauty and the Beast*—are imports from the colonies, while the homegrown productions include such luxurious twaddle as *Mamma Mia!, Bombay Dreams,* and *Starlight Express.*

Brits who view American culture with disdain are the ones who must pay the freight here, being careful not to throw stones from inside their glass houses. Though it is doubtless a bitter pill to swallow, not everything that is idiotic, pandering, or unsophisticated originated in the land of the free and the home of Kenny G. Americans did not invent *Cats*. We take no responsibility for laddie magazines. Reality TV is an import from Britain. Rupert Murdoch, though Australian, made his breakthrough on the Thames, not the Hudson. Joan and Jackie Collins are Brits. And Americans could never have invented anyone as appalling as Fergie; Streisand is the closest we get— and she's not as fat.

I suppose that I resisted the siren song of the West End for so long because even I can only stomach so much drivel. Still, it was impossible to deny: Going all the way to London without taking time out to attend a few horrendous plays was like making a special trip to Hell without ever asking to meet Satan. So this time around, I decided to plunge in headfirst. Never a fan of Noël Coward, I nonetheless reported to the

Albery Theatre, forked over a king's ransom for a good seat, and watched Alan Rickman act up a storm in *Private Lives*. Someone once said that this highly mannered actor had made a career out of being brilliant in roles where no brilliance was required. He was certainly on top of his game that evening. The play itself is one of those antediluvian titter-fests from the 1930s that continue to draw enormous crowds for no reason known to God or man. Precious and antiseptically fey, it evokes an era that never existed in a language that no one ever spoke. There are more laughs in a single act of Neil Simon than in all of Noël Coward, and I don't even like Neil Simon.

Rickman himself proved infinitely more annoying in person than he ever was on-screen—no mean feat. Frankly, it was something about the eyes. I had recently written a story for *GQ* titled "Squint While You're Ahead," paying homage to the great squinters in recent motion picture history, and even proposing an all-squinter version of *King Lear* (Helen Hunt, Jennifer Love Hewitt, Neve Campbell, Winona Ryder, Jack Nicholson, Clint Eastwood, Christian Slater, Richard Gere) with the volelike Rickman assuming the title role. Rickman was in fine optical fettle the night I watched him stroll the boards in *Private Lives;* if he ever actually opened his eyes throughout the entire performance, I never spotted it. Perhaps while I was blinking or napping.

Next on my list of self-inflicted flagellations was *The Mousetrap*. It is just barely possible to imagine a time when Agatha Christie's whodunit, playing continuously for fifty-two years, was not rickety, dull, and corny. That time would be the early eighth century, when the Venerable Bede was putting the finishing touches on his history of Saxon England. By the time *The Mousetrap* debuted in 1952, it was at least twenty years out of date, a museum piece even by the standards of Dame Agatha's stodgy, predictable craft. Today, decades after more sophisticated mysteries like *Sleuth, Deathtrap,* and even *Columbo,* it seems bewilderingly lame. An excruciatingly uninteresting two-act drama that takes place entirely in one room at a remote, snowbound country inn, *The Mousetrap* focuses on a roving strangler whose identity requires about twenty-five minutes and four brain cells to figure out. At the end of the performance, the actor playing the killer drags himself out onstage and implores the audience to keep his identity a secret, lest they spoil the show for those who have not yet attended. Since I was apparently the only person in the civilized world who had not already seen the play, this exhortation seemed entirely superfluous.

When I asked the ticket seller in the lobby how long he had been employed there, he replied that he had started out with the production thirty years ago, worked for a decade and a half, took a thirteen-year hiatus at another venue, and had only recently returned. The theater contains 552 seats, and schedules eight shows a week. Over the course of the man's seventeen-year tenure with *The Mousetrap,* this would work out to 4,400 tickets a week, 208,000 a year, approximately 3.5 million in toto. Since there are two ticket booths, let's cut that figure in half and round it off to 1.7 million. In other words, the man at the ticket office had personally had intimate social and commercial progress with more nitwits, dowagers, traveling salesmen, conventioneers, old fogies, and outright jackasses than the entire population of the City of Brotherly Love.

I sure hope his other job wasn't selling tickets to *Joseph and the Amazing Technicolor Dreamcoat.*

ONE AFTERNOON, A FRIEND INFORMED ME THAT A SUPERLA-tively horrid musical tribute to Queen had just opened at a theater on Tottenham Court Road. *We Will Rock You* was the brainchild of a middle-aged stand-up comic named Ben Elton, who had once been revered for his antiestablishment diatribes back in the Thatcher Era, but who had now joined forces with Moloch, Baal, Gog, Magog, Pluto, Lucifer, the Four Horsemen of the Apocalypse, and the long-dead but still quite dangerous Freddie Mercury to wreak havoc on the British theatrical community.

Obviously, *We Will Rock You* was a must-see. Not since I attended a Kenny G concert at Radio City Music Hall in 1997 had such an enticingly revolting specter of imbecility haunted my reveries. Nevertheless, I bided my time. My wife once explained to me that she didn't enjoy going out more than once a month because she liked to think about the upcoming concert, play, opera, or ballet and roll it over and over in her mind, and then do the same thing after the event was finished. I had a similar approach. I did not like to rush out and see the worst show in town, and very possibly on the entire planet, because once it was over months and sometimes years would pass before I stumbled upon anything similarly repellent.

The early 1990s had been a Periclean age of bad taste on both sides of the Atlantic, with *Cats, Phantom, Sunset Boulevard, Les Miz,* and *Miss Saigon* all playing simultaneously on

Broadway and in the West End; moreover, back then Billy Joel, Phil Collins, and the Grateful Dead were still going strong. But Andrew Lloyd Webber had lost his touch of late, Jerry Garcia had kicked the bucket, Billy Joel had retired, ostensibly to compose classical music, and Phil Collins had dropped off the face of the earth. London still offered lots of fifth-rate entertainment, but it did not have much in the way of *new* fifth-rate entertainment. The question in my mind was whether *We Will Rock You* could possibly live up to my dreams of gazing directly on pristine cultural excreta. The fact that it involved Queen gave me hope; if you were betting on an all-out suckfest, the good money was riding on Elton's show. But I was taking nothing for granted, having been disappointed before: Barry Manilow was nowhere near as bad as I wanted him to be when I took in his act in New York, Whoopi Goldberg was not the Antichrist I expected when I attended her Broadway debut, and Tony Orlando radiated an unexpected charm and pathos when I saw him in Branson, Missouri. This would not be the first time my dreams of total submersion in the belly of the beast had fallen short of the mark. No, indeed.

And so, just as a marathoner prepares himself for his epic undertaking by scheduling a series of short runs, I toned my psyche for the Queen extravaganza by visiting Madame Tussaud's. Madame Tussaud's is a rather large museum where people wait in line for long stretches of time to see wax renderings of Cybill Shepherd. The logic of the overpriced museum is not always in evidence. Obviously, heavyweights like Marilyn Monroe, Humphrey Bogart, and Voltaire are front and center here, but the presence and positioning of many of the figures in the venerable pop cultural institution are mystifying. For example, I can understand why Madame Tussaud's would devote precious exhibition space to John Wayne, Queen Victoria, Nelson Mandela, and Brad Pitt, but why Kwame Nkrumah? Not even people named Kwame remember what Nkrumah is famous for. A friend of mine theorizes that wax figures are so expensive to produce that the museum is reluctant to prune its holdings until a historical figure has long passed his expiration date, but I would certainly think this applies to Nkrumah. I realize that Pan-African Congress buffs will be miffed to hear this, but Kwame Nkrumah is to Nelson Mandela as Waylon Jennings is to Willie Nelson. And Jennings isn't in Madame Tussaud's. These guys are second-stringers. They're bush-leaguers. They're also-rans. They're scrubs.

That said, the single greatest problem with Madame Tussaud's is that it is insufficiently absurd. A nitpicker might object that the wax figures representing James Dean and Marlon Brando do not actually resemble them, that George Washington looks more like Billy Idol, that John Wayne is far too tall, Martin Luther King far too short, and Brad Pitt just a smidgen too simian. I personally question the proximity of Princess Diana to the pope, no less than the juxtaposition of Cybill Shepherd with Liz Taylor. Nor do I understand why Yasser Arafat has to look so happy, Muhammar Qadafi so gay, and F. W. de Klerk so harmless.

Moreover, I wish that the curators of the museum would throw the public a few more curves, like sprinkling in wax figurines of Vasco da Gama and Weezer instead of the usual suspects: Britney Spears, The Rock, Marie-Antoinette. But this is mere caviling. Madame Tussaud's is nowhere near as bad as it ought to be, and slumming tourists desperate for laughs are likely to be disappointed. I know that I was.

IN THE DAYS LEADING UP TO MY DATE WITH POP CULTURAL destiny, I was afflicted by great doubt. Physically, I was already getting the chills just thinking about how bad the Queen show might be. But a part of me worried that the musical might include some innovative, cutting-edge dancing, à la Twyla Tharp's Broadway collaboration with Billy Joel, thus mitigating the visceral effect of the Long Island schlockmeister's appalling repertory. If that were the case, it would be like hoping to catch leprosy, but instead merely coming down with a very mild, highly treatable case of bubonic plague. Here, gentle reader, I am baring my very soul: For the first time in years, I was worried.

In the end, my fears were unfounded. *We Will Rock You* is a two-and-a-half-hour musical that proceeds from the delusional premise that Queen is not the enemy. At some point in the distant future, so the story goes, all musical instruments have been destroyed by a malignant corporation that produces sappy, generic, readily downloadable music. Rebels, some dressed as punks, try to keep authentic rock 'n' roll alive by singing Queen songs. This is a curiously revisionist view of rock history. Punk, as I recall, sprang screaming from the womb in 1976, one year after Queen released "Bohemian Rhapsody." Punk, in fact, was a direct response to bands like Emerson, Lake & Palmer, Yes, Asia, the Electric Light Orchestra, and most particularly Queen, just as penicillin was a direct response to syphilis. Apparently, Ben Elton does not know this. Elton John probably does.

These delicate nuances were lost on the audience, legions of cheerful baby boomers and their maddeningly wholesome teenaged spawnlings who were too young to experience Freddie Mercury poisoning when it first afflicted the Western World. They were also lost on the feisty performers and the addled comedian who had dreamed up the show. Another of Elton's oversights was preparing a score in which both the forces of good and the forces of evil spend all their time singing Queen songs. If Queen is in fact the enemy of the GlobalSoft Corporation, then why are the employees of GlobalSoft singing Queen songs? And if the rebels are the enemies of bland music, why is their leader named Sir Paul McCartney? Riddle me that, Riddler!

I do not mean any of this as a criticism. I had come to the theater that evening seeking at least one night of entertainment that would make my stomach churn like the bowels of Saint Wulfstan. *We Will Rock You* did not disappoint. True, it was almost impossible to believe that something so triumphantly cretinous as this musical could have been manufactured without some help from Andrew Lloyd Webber, but there it was. As I sat in my orchestra seat feverishly clapping my hands to the strains of "Radio GaGa" and "Crazy Little Thing Called Love," with thousands of others joining in, I felt that I had finally plummeted into the deepest pit of the Inferno, and was now fully prepared to embrace the serpent. At long last, I felt a sense of accomplishment and a sense of closure. In the secret places of my very small heart, I had long entertained dreams of coming back in my next life as a moron.

With *We Will Rock You,* I was getting an early start.

3

I Left My Love in Avalon

There is considerable dispute as to what Thomas Gainsborough said when he shuffled off this mortal coil on August 2, 1788. Popular legend asserts that his last words were, "We are all going to Heaven, and Van Dyck is of the company." But a friend who was at his bedside when the most idiosyncratic of all English painters died reports that what he actually said was, "Van Dyck was right."

In fact, either remark would have been perfectly acceptable, even though they mean entirely different things. The first suggests that Gainsborough was reconciled to the dying of the light, as entering Paradise would enable him to meet the painter from whom he had stolen half his ideas. And the second is suitably mysterious, like Goethe crying out, "More light," or Franz Schubert inexplicably asking his landlady, "Could you be a doll and get me some more James Fenimore Cooper novels?"

But only the English would insist on *two* separate versions of Gainsborough's checkout line. Or even have the chutzpah to suggest it. Julius Caesar didn't say "Et tu, Brute?" *and* "Where's the Praetorian guard when you really need them?" John Wilkes Booth didn't shriek "*Sic semper tyrannis*" *and* "Other than that, Mrs. Lincoln, how'd you like the play?" The dueling versions of Gainsborough's final words adumbrate a central flaw in the British character. Enough is never enough. The Brits can never leave well enough alone. They always have to go overboard.

The Cult of Glastonbury is an incandescent illustration of this British anomaly. In recent years, this prosperous, yet preposterous, little town in southwestern England has become famous as the site of a summer music festival featuring such luminaries as Sting, Van Morrison, and the Pogues. But long before Sting wove his midsummer magic with songs of Tantric ardor, the city had already achieved a certain measure of celebrity. For starters, it is widely believed in these parts that after Christ's crucifixion, one of his confederates came into possession of the Holy Grail (the chalice Christ drank from on Holy Thursday) and spirited it away to Glastonbury for reasons no one has ever really tried to explain.

The man who smuggled the Grail out of Jerusalem and into Somerset is the universally admired Joseph of Arimathea, who worked in some vague capacity as a financial adviser to the Twelve Apostles during the waning days of Christ's ministry, effectively playing Engels to the Savior's Marx. There is a related tale that this enigmatic émigré and the child Christ pooled resources to build the first church in Glastonbury on the site of the now ruined abbey, despite the inherent geographical and chronological implausibilities lurking in this tale. To this day, visitors to Glastonbury can worship beneath the tree on Wearyall Hill that spontaneously sprang up when this chimerical figure stuck his staff into the ground at some point during the reign of Augustus; presumably it was later irrigated by Christ's blood. There are also rumors that Mary Magdalene, the rehabilitated tart whose alleged relationship with Jesus varies from wife to mistress to social secretary, may have passed through these parts as well. It depends on which legend you believe.

The tree ostensibly planted by Joseph of Arimathea is located not far from the ruins of Glastonbury Abbey. In its time, the abbey was the largest ecclesiastical structure in all of Britain, even roomier than the majestic Durham Cathedral. Begun in 1189, it was apparently quite well appointed, which was unfortunate because this irked the avaricious nobility, who chafed under the spiritual suzerainty of the prelates, and deeply resented the Church's domination of the pre-Renaissance real estate market. In 1539, seven years after Henry VIII made his fatal break with Rome, the abbey was plundered, its abbot executed, its monks driven out, its treasures confiscated. Some of the building's stonework later resurfaced in local homes and bridges; the rest fell into ruins.

Not terribly far from the tree planted by Joseph of Arimathea is a grave that supposedly contains the bodies of both King Arthur and his faithless wife, Lady Guinevere. King Arthur, of course, is widely reported to have lived on the craggy coast of Cornwall at Tintagel, which is nowhere near Glastonbury. Moreover, the annals of Arthurian legend specify that he was buried on an island, and there are no islands in this part of England. Guinevere's corpse has a less peripatetic mythological pedigree; she generally seems to have adhered to the code of one grave per customer. The pair were entombed in a shrine in the abbey in 1278, then vanished after the building was destroyed. They reappeared in 1934, during an archaeological dig that had nothing to do with them. They go in and out of fashion, skipping town for centuries at a time before miraculously putting in a fresh appearance. The fact that both Arthur's and Guinevere's reasonably well-preserved bodies unexpectedly crashed the party in 1191 in the midst of a monastic fund-raising drive after a fire had destroyed the original abbey also encourages doubting Thomases to take this highly suspicious medieval mortician's yarn with a grain of salt.

But what the calculating monks of that era seemed to understand is that a myth has to start *somewhere,* so you might as well give it a go. All of the great national myths—Roland, El Cid, Saint George—were cooked up in the late feudal periods as public relations materials useful in recasting assorted polyglot communities into a single nation. When these myths were first promulgated, most thinking people recognized that they were hoaxes. The problem was, in the late Middle Ages, there weren't very many thinking people, as most people were serfs or lepers; moreover, the thinking people were the ones concocting the myths, as they were useful in getting poor people to go off and fight pointless foreign wars, thus holding down crime and unemployment. With the passage of time, even the least plausible myths take on a certain legitimacy—George Washington chopping down the cherry tree, Caesar crossing the Rubicon, Moses conversing with the Burning Bush, Diogenes telling Alexander the Great to move just a few inches to the right because he was blocking the light. When lies are new, they are called myths. When lies are old, they become history.

Here's a question worth pondering: Is there *any* place in Britain where Arthur isn't buried? The aforementioned myth puts him in Glastonbury. Another has him in Cornwall. The Scots will direct you to a crag called King Arthur's Seat in Edinburgh, which may contain all or part of his remains, and I once read a letter to the editor in *The Stroud News and Journal* wherein a local screwball claimed to have definitive proof that Camelot was located in nearby Woodchester. Just about the only place Arthur doesn't seem to be buried is Blackpool, because it wouldn't do to have his shriveled corpse resurface in a Butlin's somewhere. For someone who almost certainly never lived, King Arthur turns up in an awful lot of final resting places.

YOU WOULD THINK THAT WITH ITS COPIOUS PAELLA OF BOGUS and legitimate history, Glastonbury could ease up on the accelerator. But no, there are also rumors that Saint Patrick operated in the district back in the fifth century. And lurid tales of prehistoric fertility rites. And, oh yes, legends of the Knights Templar. Personally, I have never been put off by the implausible myth of Merlin or the equally suspect tale of the Sword in the Stone. The Lady of the Lake, the legend of Sir Galahad, and Parsifal's quest for the Holy Grail I'm fine with, and for all I know the original Round Table from Camelot may very well be in present use as a serving board at

the tapas bar at the Savoy Grill. But as soon as anyone men-
tions Jacques de Molay and the Knights Templar, I ask for my
check and leave. Ditto the Rosicrucians. There's only so far I
can be pushed.

Why would an undeniably resplendent town, so lavishly
endowed with a cornucopia of vaguely credible folktales, risk
all of its municipal credibility on these repeated rolls of the
mythological dice? Simple: The Brits always want more. It's
not enough to have the legend of Pete Best; they also insist on
the legend of Stu Sutcliffe. It's not enough that Henry VIII
had a wife with three breasts and eleven fingers; there also
has to be a theory that he was responsible for the invention of
extrawide shoes and composed "Greensleeves." It's not
enough that Queen Elizabeth was the most famous virgin
potentate in history; there also has to be a story that she was
Shakespeare's mistress, or the mother of Francis Bacon (who
may have written Shakespeare's plays), or was abducted in the
West Country while still a girl and replaced by a boy who
must have had a rollicking old time gamboling in the sack
with Essex, Sir Walter Raleigh, and the Earl of Dudley, who
may have been his or her son. It's not enough to claim that
Stonehenge was built by the Druids; there also has to be a
theory that Avebury was built by the Egyptians. It's not
enough to claim that Boadicea vanished after the cataclysmic
defeat of the Iceni in A.D. 60; there also has to be a report that
her body resides beneath one of the commuter platforms at
King's Cross train station.

For similar reasons, the English insist on perpetuating the
legend that Richard II was never formally executed but gnawed
himself to death in Pontefract Castle. Or that Edward II

escaped being impaled on a red-hot poker by persuading a late-medieval stool pigeon to sit in for him, and spent the rest of his life in Sicily, cavorting with supple catamites. Or that Horatio Nelson was pickled in 157 bottles of brandy after Trafalgar, that his corpse was then smuggled back into England, and that the entire crew drank a toast to him, quaffing the jaunty embalming fluid. Most societies would be more than happy just to have Jack the Ripper in the starting lineup, but the English insist on cooking up a legend that the fiendish murderer was a member of the royal family, or a semifamous painter, or Rudyard Kipling on boys' night out (only joking).

Even though the Brits know that they have everyone else hopelessly outgunned in the department of mythological savagery, they cannot resist pouring it on. The Romans specialized in crucifixions; the ancient Germans once suspended thousands of Roman survivors of the Battle of Teutoburg Forest in baskets and set them on fire. Shaka Zulu regularly impaled captives on sharp stakes and Genghis Khan is reputed to have dined on a makeshift box containing the slowly suffocating sultan who had dared to defy him. The Vikings were masters of the blood-eagle, the Aztecs tried to placate their insatiable gods by sacrificing cooperative virgins in the thousands, but nobody ever did a better job at torturing their political and religious adversaries than the English.

The English were so good at this sort of thing, and practiced it with such shocking frequency, that many men who were hanged, drawn, quartered, and disemboweled have receded into the mists of history without getting their proper due. Saint John Southworth, whose remains are enshrined in

Westminster Cathedral, a Catholic institution just a hop, skip, and a jump from Victoria Station, was the last secular priest to be executed in this extravagantly barbarous fashion. Condemned to death in 1654, he was so well liked that the judge who passed the sentence burst into tears as he pronounced it. After his death, the four quarters of his body were allegedly sewn back together and removed to Douay, in Catholic France. When Douay was destroyed during the French Revolution, the saint's remains, not unlike those of King Arthur, disappeared for several centuries, not reappearing until 1927. A few years later, they were transported to the Chapel of St. George at Westminster Cathedral, where they abide today.

The skeptic in me has several reservations about this legend. Who were the seamstresses who reassembled Southworth's mangled corpse? What kind of training did they have? How much were they paid? Do we know that they got the pieces back in the right order? Did anyone check? Is there a chance that some of the fragments belonged to Saint John Southworth, but that the rest were the remains of other victims that happened to be lying around that day? And can we be absolutely sure that when the body parts were rediscovered in 1927, this was not just another French prank? It would not be beyond them; the puckishness of the Gauls knows no bounds.

Perhaps the most interesting thing about all this is that the legend of Saint John Southworth is not widely known. I had never heard of him before I visited the cathedral in London, and I have a kind of hobbyist's sixth sense about these things. It is a testament to the zeal and frequency with which the

English carried out such ferocious mutilations—which served as a form of public entertainment—that Saint John Southworth is no more than a footnote to history. In a mythology-challenged society like New Zealand or Costa Rica, Southworth would be a huge, huge star. In Britain, he is merely a spare part, a benchwarmer. But he is there, just in case the Brits ever need him.

Historical overkill of this sort never ceases. Consider the chapter in Peter Ackroyd's encyclopedic *London: The Biography* where he asserts that the original Westminster Abbey, conceived by Saint Edward the Confessor (a fat, passive albino) shortly before the Norman Conquest, "became the repository of sand from Mount Sinai and earth from Calvary, a beam from the Holy Manger of Jesus and pieces of His cross, blood from Christ's side and milk from the Virgin Mary, a finger from St. Paul and hair from St. Peter." *What!* No mildewed joists from the workshop of Joseph the Carpenter? No tarnished goblets from the Marriage Feast at Cana? No rancid halibut left over from the miracle of the loaves and fishes? And you call *that* a relics collection?

Ackroyd, of course, exhumes the hoary myth that London was founded by refugees from Troy. Though he concedes that most historians dismiss this theory as fraudulent, he suggests that Brutus, the great-grandson of Aeneas, who founded Rome, may be buried on Tower Hill, having reached the shores of Albion sometime around 1100 B.C. Ackroyd goes on and on about the stone of Brutus, which until recently could be seen on Charing Cross Road in central London. He even hypothesizes that the "famous British motif comprising the lion and the unicorn may be of Chaldean origin," suggesting that the English are descended from the Assyrians. In making this assertion, he cites no less an authority than Diogenes Laertius.

I don't give a tinker's damn what Diogenes Laertius has to say about the Assyrian Chaldeans; I think all this Trojan chatter is blarney. Once the English got their empire up and running, they were desperate to forge a mythological link with all the great civilizations of the past because they couldn't abide the fact that the country was almost certainly founded by the Celts, who were just a little bit too close to the Irish for comfort. That is their prerogative. But I personally do not think this is fair. The British already have Boadicea, King Arthur, Lancelot du Lac, Merlin, Lady Godiva, Richard the Lion-Hearted, Harold of Wessex, Thomas à Becket, the Lion in Winter, Hotspur, Good Queen Bess, Mary, Queen of Scots, Bloody Mary, Guy Fawkes, the Duke of Wellington, Horatio Nelson, Oliver Cromwell, Winston Churchill, Montgomery of El Alamein, and John Major. Frankly, I think that's more than enough. It's unfair to go rooting about in other civilizations' cultural attics; it smacks of the greed and tackiness the rest of the world associates with Americans.

Purporting to be descended from the Trojans when you already claim to be descended from the Druids is like Americans claiming that Baton Rouge was founded by Charlemagne, or that Hector Berlioz wrote "Oh! Susanna" under an assumed name, or that Saint Francis of Assisi, Diocletian, Franz Josef Haydn, and Kublai Khan grew up in what is now Kokomo, Indiana. The whole notion of London as a new Troy founded by a distant relative of Hector (who was in no position to found anything after Achilles mopped the floor with him) is yet another example of the British penchant for overdoing everything. Before I depart this vale of sorrows, I would love to see this insanity stop. It's unseemly and vulgar, and it makes the entire nation seem like it's suffering from a massive insecurity complex. So here is my advice to the fabulists of Great Britain and the well-meaning numskulls that encourage them: Lay off. Calm down. Get a grip. As for you, Mr. Ackroyd, *knock it off*.

GIVEN ITS PSEUDOMYTHICAL HISTORY—CHRIST AND MARY Magdalene, Arthur and Guinevere, Henry VIII and Anne Boleyn, Sting and Sinéad O'Connor—downtown Glastonbury has gradually evolved into a Mecca for out-and-out lunatics. The streets are filled with shops named The Goddess and the Green Man, Man, Myth & Magik, The Crystal Star, Healing Hearts, and The Sufi Charity Shop, which must be doing a roaring business these days. These are supplemented by The Speaking Tree, Gothic Image, Yin-Yang Health & Harmony, The Psychic Piglet, and Dilliway & Dilliway (formerly Dragons). Glastonburgundians sport more graying ponytails and lurid peasant dresses than you can shake a stick at, and that's just the men. Ambling down the streets of this Town That Time Forgot But The Body Shop Didn't, you feel as if the entire population of Haight-Ashbury had ripped a page from Joseph of Arimathea's book back in the Summer of Love and hotfooted it to Glastonbury en masse. Everyone looks like they've just stepped out of a Dante Gabriel Rossetti painting that he never got around to finishing because even he knew it was too over the top.

It goes without saying that Glastonbury is filled with shops selling amulets and incense burners and sacred stones and printed matter imbued with the kind of runic, fortune cookie sagacity that used to be a staple of Procol Harum albums. One store has a sign reading:

KINDNESS IS MORE IMPORTANT THAN WISDOM;

RECOGNITION OF THIS IS THE BEGINNING OF WISDOM.

I have never found this to be the case. I've gotten this far being wise without being kind, and my feeling is: If it ain't broke don't fix it. Clearly, this is not my kind of town. It's the kind of town where you are actually happy to see a battalion of soccer hooligans show up; where you feel solidarity with the acne-plagued skateboarders. Outside the Glastonbury Healing Center, a withered crone, detecting my spiritual malaise, suggested that I try an exotic, spiritual massage fortified with myriad herbal elements, probably endorsed by both the National Health and Merlin. (The single biggest difference between Great Britain and the United States is that in all of our history, and even in the history of the dreamy, peyote-smoking aboriginals we displaced, we never produced anyone like Merlin. The closest we got was Shirley MacLaine.)

"I'm sorry, that won't work for me," I replied. "I'm from Philadelphia."

Readers who have seen *The Ring*, particularly the original Japanese version, have probably spent many sleepless nights alone in a remote cottage terrified that the footpad they just heard on the stairs is the dead girl with the purple skin who slithers out of the television set at the end of the film. The girl is admittedly gruesome, but she is a chubby-cheeked cherub compared to the Tony Blair Witch Projectiles you come across in Glastonbury. Inside the Lady Chapel at the abbey, I spotted a thirtyish woman with plaited hair, an American Eagle sweater, a flowing peasant dress, and combat boots kneeling in a profound trance, her eyes riveted on something so mystically proto-Celtic no one else could see it. She looked oddly familiar, though I could not immediately place her face. Then it came to me: She bore an astonishing resemblance to Medusa. Yes, this astral lassie was *really* scary; I hadn't seen that haunted, drug-addled look up close and personal since Black Sabbath did a triple bill with Tull and King Crimson at the Fillmore East in 1971. It was time to get the hell out of there and beat a hasty retreat to the Excalibur Café.

No observer worth his salt, or even somebody else's salt, can deny that eccentricity is the coin of the realm in Britain. But the other side of the coin is an omnivorous cuteness that devours everything in its path. In York one March morning, I took a spot of refreshment in a gorgeous little tea shop situated on a bridge that joins the old city with the new. Arrayed around the dainty little shop were fey promotional materials referring to an even more ancient establishment called The Ness Café. Get it? Ness? Café? According to this reading material, Lucy Luckett, founder of the York-based tea shop, "had visited the Scottish highlands to recuperate after a particularly arduous season at court." *Garçon! I'll take some twee with my tea!* Subsequently, according to the same local legend, Lady Luckett visited The Ness Café, a tea shop founded by an Oriental named Mr. Phoo, who taught her son "the secrets of many mariners' knots, thereby earning the boy the nickname of 'Tie.'" As in Ty-Phoo, the tea. *Are the pieces of the puzzle starting to come together?* There was also a line about Lucy opening her tea shop "to the alarm of many peacocks . . . but that's another tail . . ."

This kind of neo–Beatrix Potterian fiddle-dee-dee makes my blood boil. It's not enough that you're running a gorgeous little tea shop. It's not enough that the tea shop is situated on a bridge that straddles a river, boasting a gracious architectural style that went out of fashion centuries ago. It's not enough that the bridge is located in one of the most beautiful cities in all of Europe. No, the Pumblechookian bloodlust for bloviating preciousness that burns in so many Britons' blood impels otherwise sensible human beings to pile it on with Mr. Phoo, the mysterious Highlanders, and the Loch Ness monster. The British have already cornered the market on history; they've already cornered the market on eccentricity; they've already cornered the market on romance; so now they want to go and corner the market on choochiness.

Speaking of the Highlanders, let us review the suspect saga of Greyfriars Bobby. The Greyfriars Church in Edinburgh is celebrated in its own right as a historically significant house of worship, containing as it does a memorial to the Scottish religious leaders martyred during "the Killing Time" of the late 1600s. But to tweeness buffs it is even more famous as the home of Greyfriars Bobby, a faithful pooch who loved his master so much that after the man died in 1858, he curled up and slept on his grave every night for fourteen years until he too finally keeled over. No matter how hard it was raining, sleeting, or hailing, Bobby would not take cover inside the church. Today, a statue and fountain in honor of the devoted

Skye terrier stand in the church graveyard, designed by no less a personage than Baroness Burdett-Coutts.

One evening I had a bit of time on my hands, so I visited the graveyard just as the moon was chasing away the sun (around three in the afternoon in late-winter Scotland). Though raised as a Catholic, and therefore reasonably credulous, I absolutely refuse to believe that this incident ever happened. I think that local cornballs murdered the dog and deposited its corpse on its master's grave in a frantic effort to vault Edinburgh to global supremacy in the rarefied world of nineteenth-century mawkishness. Dogs simply don't do things like curl up and die because they pine for their master; hand them a mouthful of raw sirloin or even a half-eaten squirrel and they'd rip their own mother to pieces. The legend of Greyfriars Bobby is like the legend of Seabiscuit: a cunning ruse cooked up by the government to make poor people feel better about themselves without actually seeing their condition materially improved. I hate Lassie. I dislike Rin-Tin-Tin. I think St. Bernards are idiotic. I am not all that taken with the Queen's corgis. I did not enjoy *101 Dalmations*.

But I *loathe* Greyfriars Bobby.

My wife, who is neither choochy nor twee, is always complaining that I confuse the two terms. Mind you, she is the kind of person who maintains a museum of singed tea cozies, smuggles Devonshire clotted cream through U.S. customs at risk of deportation, and says things like "more's the pity," "coals to Newcastle," and "you've taken the king's shilling." She is also rather fond of sarnies and bickies. So she may not be the best person to ask. In any event, I disagree with her verdict. Choochiness is yet another British term that has no precise meaning, but, like pornography, you know it when you see it. The way I have things stacked up, choochiness is a particularly British amalgam of cuddlywuddliness, cutesy-piedness, and butter-wouldn't-melt-in-my-mouthedness that embraces everything from shops named The Ketch to Hugh Grant's stammer. It is a grating and often maddening behavioral pattern that makes others want to reach out and pinch the choochster's cheeks while secretly longing to stuff a hand grenade right down his throat.

"Paul McCartney is choochy; John Lennon is not," says my brother-in-law, Max, who fled England for France in 1976, largely to escape from rampant choochiness. "Paul McCartney: choochy. John Lennon: not choochy. That's the difference."

THERE IS A THEORY IN CERTAIN QUARTERS THAT KOREAN grocers who have immigrated to the United States deliberately misspell their fruit and vegetable signs because they believe that Americans find this vaguely charming. I feel the same way about names like Bumble's Tea Room and Sally Slapcabbage: Handmade Local Crafts. It's all a con job, possibly bankrolled by descendants of the Krays, secretly planning to seize control of every wee little tea shop in the UK and use them as money-laundering operations. I don't mind pubs with names like The Noose & Monkey or The Tilted Wig or The Parson's Buttocks, but I don't want to hear some glib, gnostic tale about the history of the establishments, and I don't want anyone thinking that they're putting something over on me. True, we do occasionally get this sort of thing in the Housatonic valley of Connecticut and the rolling hills of the Berkshires in Massachusetts, where a wrong turn may find you stumbling upon entire Brigadoonish villages teeming with belligerently genteel craft shops. But at least no one tries to pretend that The Antic Cobbler or The Improvident Patroon date from the time of Paul Revere. Most of them were founded in 1994 by somebody named Weiss, O'Shaughnessy, or Siemenkowski.

How can you tell when you have crossed the Threshold of Tweeness, passed through the Portals of Ponciness, and officially entered the fair bower of Countie Chooch? One telltale sign is when someone says it's a shame you weren't here last week for the annual Furry Dance. Another is when a volunteer from the local museum hands you a flyer announcing "The Great Mug Appeal," and requests not only that you fork over your beloved drinking ware but that you supply any personal anecdotes and recollections explaining why this particular item is so important to you. ("I koshed Phil Collins with it, then used the jagged edges to tear his eyes out of their sockets.") Perhaps the surest indication that you have wandered into the Vale of the Choochy Piglet, where Winnie-the-Pooh, Tigger, and Christopher Robin await you, with Noddy, Thumper, Peter and Cottontail, and a phalanx of Wombles lurking in a nearby copse, is when you find yourself in a glorified alley and spot a grubby little cottage called The Rookery, Moonfleet, or Dream Achieved. The hovel in question is a disintegrating little semidetached on a back street in a dismal provincial town; what kind of dream is *that*? It would be as if people in El Paso started naming their glorified Quonset huts Escorial, The Alhambra, or Casa de los Reyes. *Spy* magazine once ran an article delving into the question of whether has-beens like Robert Goulet knew how preposterous they had become. Some did; some didn't; but most of them honestly believed that their sun had merely gone into momentary eclipse. For similar reasons, I have always longed to find out if people living in pokey little cottages named Nuage Argentée are serious, delusional, or merely having the public on. For their sake, I hope they are simply taking the mickey.

One question that has long perplexed me is whether choochiness is a strand of cultural DNA that is genetically transmitted from one generation to the next. Clearly, certain national characteristics—twittishness, studious reserve, miserliness—have an enduring quality and are not confined to a single generation. The felons who trail Manchester United from Barcelona to Malta are obviously the descendants of the thugs who conquered India and the Sudan. The simpering toff with the swish scarf who seeks to borrow fifteen quid so he can buy a magenta dickey that once belonged to Frank Capra is indisputably a direct descendant of Beau Brummell, who refused to lead his troops from London to quell a riot in Manchester because "a gentleman does not go to Manchester." Margaret Thatcher claims direct psychological lineage from both Queen Elizabeth and Oliver Cromwell; Neil Kinnock is the spiritual heir of the ineffectual eighteenth-century Whigs who literally spent decades out of power. Churchill was not the first Brit with a stiff upper lip; the blood of Caractacus ran right through his veins. But what of the choochsters? Is choochiness something that will one day die out in Britain? Will middle-class women ever stop talking like Felicity Kendal? Will Felicity

Kendall? Will Sally Slapcabbage ever stop slapping her cabbage? Will the proprietors of the Ness Café one day elect to put Lucy Luckett out to pasture and replace her with Ilsa, She-Bitch of Yorkshire?

I have no way of knowing. But one thing is certain: Choochiness can strike anywhere, at any time of day or night. One evening, when I attended a panel on journalism convened in a York theater, a furloughed human interest columnist from Leeds got up and read an interminable story about a sweet little pooch having a tidy wee in the garden. *Ladies and gentlemen, put your hands together and give it up for Mrs. Piddly-Tinkle!* The compact, belligerently harmless woman seemed astonished that the barbaric new owners of the newspaper had laid her column to rest, while simultaneously confessing that she had "no buzz for news." As if puppies peeing in the shimmering gardens of South Yorkshire were not newsworthy! She concluded her hypnotically juvenile presentation with a poem discussing her career woes, now that she could no longer make a living writing about heartwarming canine urinary exploits. The final lines ran like this:

I'm a broadsheet woman in a tabloid town
And I'm waitin' in the shadows till the sun comes down.

To which I can only reply:

I'm a mean-assed Yank and I got no class;
But I hope some honey bunny kicks your ass.

4

Oh Christ, Not the Mill *and* the Floss!

Writers, and even ordinary mortals, love to wax philosophic about the books that shaped their intellects. Invariably, by some meretricious act of retroactive precocity, they insist that their lives were changed forever by their exposure to *Pride and Prejudice, Don Quixote, The Idiot,* or *Madame Bovary,* which they read at age nine. I for one am fond of telling people that the book that first sculpted my worldview was Immanuel Kant's *Prolegomena to Any Future Metaphysics.* In fact, I have never read it. The only reason I have masqueraded for so long as a kindergarten Kantian is because I am a member of the very last generation of Americans that thought you could impress women by using words like *prolegomena.*

As a writer, I would love to report that the authors who sparked my lifelong love affair with the English language—and literature itself—were the titans of British fiction. In doing so, I would be imitating some of my closest friends.

One of my colleagues has read *Pride and Prejudice* nine times, claiming to pinpoint in its coy prose the very key to the relationship between men and women. On three distinct occasions I have briefly fallen in with G. K. Chesterton buffs who took up the cudgels in defense of "the most overlooked prose stylist of the past hundred years." Once I even had lunch with a troika of bond traders and financiers who covetously groped a metal key that allegedly belonged to the author of the Father Brown books. No post-Edwardian crime fiction buff, I felt like Judas skulking in the cenacle. My daughter's fourth-grade teacher once spent a week in Oxford holed up in the house where Lewis Carroll wrote *Alice in Wonderland*. I have also crossed both paths and swords with persnickety members of the Baker Street Irregulars, intrepid voyagers to Cawdor Castle, and legions of writers who feel compelled to visit Stratford-on-Avon and draw inspiration from the Immortal Bard. As if that would improve their prose.

I will not deny that I myself have occasionally engaged in similar pilgrimages of this nature. I once visited Manchester just to see if it was as deadly as A. J. P. Taylor said it was. (I was only there for an evening, but sensed that the great popular historian and disgruntled Manchester native was onto something. Young people insist that there are lots of things to do in Manchester, but mostly what they do is ecstasy.) I also made a special trip to a house outside St. Ives where Virginia Woolf used to wander down from London on the weekends foraging for pocket-sized rocks. Over the years I have come to know and love most, if not all, of the British masters (Thackeray, Tennyson, and Hardy still elude me; Lawrence is an acquired taste I have taken great pains not to acquire; and I loathe Restoration comedy, though it is certainly a vast improvement over Puritan comedy). That said, I cede pride of place to no man in my admiration for Dickens, Shaw, Wilde, Fielding, Boswell, Eliot, Sterne, Smollett, and assorted Brontës and Amises. Still, it would be churlish not to admit that these appetites blossomed rather late in life, and that I, like most American schoolchildren, grew up despising, nay *dreading*, them all.

When I was a youngster, educated by bellicose nuns in parochial schools in the City of Brotherly Love, British literature functioned almost entirely as a punitive pedagogical mechanism. American children were compelled to study authors they could neither understand nor enjoy, simply because these giants were indisputably *moral*. Though we were *never, ever* taken to art museums to gaze at the works of the Great Masters, and were never required to listen to classical music, as the Catholic Church doesn't approve of that sort of thing, we were compelled to memorize poems like "Lochinvar" and "On First Looking into Chapman's Homer," and commanded to hack our way through daunting novels like *David Copperfield, The Mill on the Floss, The Return of the Native,* and *Persuasion.* One of the least understood forms of child abuse, Outstanding British Literature wrecked our Yuletide holidays and summer vacations and made us grow up loathing highbrow fiction.

In fairness, this brutally uncompromising regimen of British classics was supplemented by comparable North American Horrors like *Moby-Dick, The Last of the Mohicans, The House of the Seven Gables,* and *The Old Man and the Sea.*

But at least with the American authors we had a fighting chance of poleaxing our way through to chapter 2. James Fenimore Cooper had his fiendish Indians; Nathaniel Hawthorne had his ghosts and witches; and Hemingway's geriatric *Jaws: The Prequel* made few demands on the unformed mind, holding out at least a flickering hope that some determined shark might finally put the protagonist out of his misery. Ditto Melville, though with a whale. The Brits offered no such respites from gravitas. It was all the flutter of crinoline, the scent of wisteria. God, how we hated them!

A great man once said that a classic was a book you wanted somebody else to read for you. Or a book that you wanted to have already read. Or words to that effect; perhaps the man was not so great after all. What is definitely true about the British classics is that they were never meant to be read by children. Especially American children. They are too long; they are too complicated; they are too depressing; and they have too many characters named Gradgrind. Reading the classics was always a bitter chore and anyone who says that he was smitten by *The Barchester Towers* or *Le Morte d'Arthur* before hitting the age of thirty is a liar. There are many of these liars about; a fair few teach literature. But if a writer is honest about the authors who first influenced him, it is almost always the odd, the quirky, the justifiably forgotten, or the just plain awful that come to the fore.

At a very early age, I became aware that Great British Literature breaks down into three broad groups: books that are very depressing, books in which nothing happens, and books that are incomprehensible. The first group includes all of Thomas Hardy, the Brontës, and most of Charles Dickens.

The second group comprises the work of George Eliot, William Thackeray, and Jane Austen. The third group consists of hoary antiques like *Beowulf*, the *Canterbury Tales*, and the plays of Ben Jonson, none of which can be understood without enormous amounts of supplementary reading of books written by people who are even more cryptic than Ben Jonson, Chaucer, and whoever wrote *Beowulf*. Obviously, none of these groups are hermetically sealed: The novels of Joseph Conrad and Virginia Woolf are both depressing *and* incomprehensible, and nothing ever happens in any of their works. And some of Dickens's novels are less lugubrious than others; I always found his cartoonish portrayal of the French Revolution a bit of a hoot, and as Oscar Wilde sagaciously quipped, one must have a heart of stone not to laugh at the plight of Little Nell.

C. S. Lewis asserts that we read to know that we are not alone, but the fact is that youngsters often are alone, frequently stuck with a book by C. S. Lewis. The child views literature as an ordeal that must be survived, like a boiler explosion or rabies; he is a shipwrecked sailor cast adrift on the Wide Sargasso Sea scanning the horizon for a cabin cruiser that might be carrying a couple of well-thumbed Philip K. Dick novels. Growing up in a grim North Philadelphia housing project with an alcoholic father and a cadre of pyromaniac playmates, I did not find *Oliver Twist* particularly inspirational, as the monstrous Fagin and Bill Sikes were no worse than the thugs who lived down the street, or most of my uncles. Many years later, I would come to understand that the popularity of *Oliver Twist* had helped to bring about much-needed social reforms in Victorian London.

Unfortunately, I was not living in Victorian London; I was living in postwar Philadelphia, where the underlying message of Dickens's work had yet to gain purchase. Today, similarly puzzled black children languishing in dismal inner-city slums are required to read *To Kill a Mockingbird,* and must wonder, "How come *we* never get to meet anybody like Atticus Finch?"

Bound spread-eagled on the roasting coals of Great British Literature while still a meek, vulnerable adolescent, I began to think of high school reading requirements as a brutal military campaign. The advance guard (A. E. Housman, William Blake, John Donne) first appeared on the foreboding bluffs to the left. Arrayed on the starboard side were William Wordsworth, Robert Browning, and Richard Sheridan. Suddenly, the onslaught was unleashed, with all three Brontës brandishing their fearsome battle-axes. Having already survived a flanking action by Samuel Taylor Coleridge and Jane Austen, I was now forced to battle the pitiless oppressors to a fare-thee-well. But just when it seemed the attack might be repelled, the Redcoats wheeled up the siege guns (Chaucer, Milton, Shakespeare, Dickens). Now, all avenues of retreat were cut off by George Bernard Shaw, E. M. Forster, and the ferociously cruel Gerard Manley Hopkins. Forced to surrender, survivors were dragged in fetters to the death camps where John Keats, Percy Bysshe Shelley, John Dryden, and Alexander Pope sat sharpening their knives. Then, next semester, the ordeal started all over again with Philip Sidney, Edmund Spenser, and Algernon Swinburne. The Brits were merciless—and they just kept coming.

■ ■ ■

PEOPLE LOVE TO TALK ABOUT THE "SPECIAL RELATIONSHIP" that characterizes Anglo-American social congress, but I think it's bunk. The British lost the Revolutionary War, capriciously resumed hostilities in the War of 1812, surreptitiously backed the Confederacy during the Civil War, and almost came to blows with the United States over Canada on several occasions. The British have always looked down their noses at their American "cousins"; to this day, they think we are vulgar, loud, coarse, and acquisitive. Where they get that idea, I'll never know. Born cheapskates, Brits come to America and make a special point of visiting hellholes like Niagara Falls, Orlando, Florida, and Times Square, merely to reinforce their worst prejudices against Americans. They have never truly approved of us; they do not really feel comfortable in our company: Gullible Americans always mistake their manicured civility for affection.

Americans, for their part, have always resented British haughtiness. There is nothing worse than being looked at down the nose by somebody who paid less for the nose job. We took forever to get into the First World War, robbed the Brits blind with the Lend-Lease Act, did not enter the Second World War until the Battle of Britain was over, screwed our best friends during the Suez Crisis, and most recently stabbed Tony Blair in the back over Iraq. As A. J. P. Taylor once noted, Franklin Delano Roosevelt personally supervised the dismantlement of the British Empire and then made the British pick up the tab for the catastrophe. The long and the short of it is:

We use Britain for our needs, and Britain uses us for hers. True, we like each other a lot more than either of us likes the French, Germans, or Japanese. But who wouldn't?

If there is a special relationship between Great Britain and the United States, it is cultural. We gave you Elvis and Chuck Berry; you gave us the Beatles and the Rolling Stones. We exported 77 *Sunset Strip* and *The Twilight Zone*; you shipped back *The Avengers* and *The Prisoner*. More recently, you gave us *The Full Monty, Brassed Off, Billy Elliot, Little Voice, Bend It Like Beckham, Saving Grace,* and *Calendar Girls,* all of which are basically the same movie, while we gave you *The Matrix, The Matrix Reloaded, The Matrix Revolutions, The Matrix European Vacation, When Harry Met the Matrix, Boyz in the Matrix,* and *Matrixes of New York.* Yet an even stronger bond lies in the nagging sense of shared adolescent literary misfortune. We both had to suffer through Thomas Hardy's *Return of the Native;* we both had to hack our way through *Jude the Obscure;* we were both force-fed *Middlemarch;* we both had to endure Maggie Tulliver's travails both *in* the Mill and *on* the Floss. Your childhood was traumatized by Alfred Lord Tennyson and William Blake, but so was ours; we were brutalized as teens by Elizabeth Barrett Browning and Rudyard Kipling, but so were you. No wonder so many adults on both sides of the Atlantic end up reading, and seemingly enjoying, butchers like Stephen King and Tom Clancy. We are constantly striving to recapture the blissful childhood we were denied because we had to spend so much of our youth reading *Heart of Darkness.* And a large part of being a happy child is being an illiterate.

Joseph Conrad has always occupied a special place in my

rogues' gallery of cultural villains. Born in Poland in 1857, Conrad wrote prose as if he'd never left home. Given to tortuous plot structures and a penchant for narrators who seemed to be missing a few screws, Conrad possessed an almost supernatural inability to come to the point. His sentences are so labyrinthine, so fiendishly devoid of logic, he makes late Henry James read like *Spot Among the Corgis*. My personal Conradian beef stems from the fact that I have never been able to give up on a book once I have started it, even if I must come back to it years after setting it aside. It took me three years to finish Ford Madox Ford's *The Good Soldier*. It took me eleven years to get through *Wuthering Heights*. But that was child's play compared to *Lord Jim;* I started reading it shortly after Freddie and the Dreamers' first single was released in 1963 and did not polish it off until 2003.

Conrad's classic is a masterpiece of obtuseness, satanically designed to frustrate the reader at every turn. It starts out as a simple tale of a sailor who deserts his post during an apparent shipwreck and must endure the stigma of this dastardly act for the remainder of his days. But a few chapters into the proceedings, Conrad maliciously introduces a narrator named Marlowe, who may or may not be the same Marlow who made *Heart of Darkness* such a personal Calvary for so many high school seniors. Virtually the entire novel is presented as a gabfest among wizened old salts, with quotes jammed inside quotes, and other quotes inserted inside those quotes, making it impossible to figure out who is talking to whom. Not to mention the fact that Conrad never addresses the question of why a bunch of liquored-up pukka sahibs perching on a sweltering balcony in the Siam of yore would have been willing to sit still and listen to this bilious old gasbag rattling on and on about some lily-livered sap they didn't even know, much less care about.

Then, just when it seems that the reader might be able to get a handle on the story line, Conrad capriciously introduces several additional structural obstructions: long-lost letters, mysterious diaries, the nineteenth-century equivalent of blogs. As luridly depressing as *Wuthering Heights*, with an even more convoluted narrative scaffolding, *Lord Jim* is almost certainly the reason Ernest Hemingway introduced his idiotic baby talk in *A Farewell to Arms*. Hemingway, for all his faults, understood that the novelist has to give the reader a fighting chance of understanding what in tarnation is going on. Otherwise, literature, like war, is hell.

AS AN IMPOVERISHED YOUNG AMATEUR DETERMINED TO become a rich old professional, what I first sought in litera-ture was the quality of mercy. I wasn't looking for inspiration; I was looking for an even break. Like a plot. And at least one character who did not carry a snuff box. The first great British writer I did not explicitly dread was Sir Walter Scott, whose classic *Ivanhoe* I gobbled up when I was fourteen years old. *Ivanhoe* is Scott's Industrial Age attempt to create a medieval national epic, weaving together the disparate legends of Robin Hood and Richard the Lion-Hearted in an effort to explain how the vanquished Saxons subtly undermined the cultural influence of the victorious Normans. (Edward I, born in 1239, was the first post-invasion king to speak English as his native language.) Unlike Dickens, Austen, Eliot, and

Hardy, who used the newly invented novel to illuminate social and economic inequities in Victorian England, Scott used the novel to help people forget their jobs.

Scott is at pains to explain that while most Normans were bad (they were French, of course), some Normans were good (Richard I and his hell-for-leather entourage). *Ivanhoe* is filled with zany remarks like "By the soul of Hengist!" and "The curse of St. Withold upon these infernal porkers!" and is unarguably the precursor of *Lord of the Rings* and *The Hobbit*. (Yes, Scott has much to answer for.) Ruffians and rustic hinds with earthy names like Wamba, Gurth, and Higg, the Son of Snell regularly burst out with such unexpectedly oracular statements as "Hasty hand catches frog for fish" and "By the scallopshells of Compostella!," worrying all the while that they will be disparaged as meddlesome coxcombs. Needless to say, jousters in the lists of Ashby-de-la-Zouche sport archaic names like the Knight of the Fetterlock; they are decked out cap-a-pie in cuirasses and chain-mail singlets borrowed from Reuben of Tadcaster, brandishing resplendent shields bearing the motto "Cave, Adsum," which they had recently hoisted in resisting "the saber of the Mosemah," whoever they were.

Ivanhoe also contains macabre supplementary materials in which Scott meticulously describes how hapless Saxon noblemen were roasted alive on massive gridirons to loosen their tongues regarding the whereabouts of the booty of Brian de Bois-Guilbert or any other booty that happened to be lying around. This made them extremely wroth, as they had to spend the rest of their lives wandering around the Kingdom by the Sea looking like partially cooked partridges. Jeepers! This was the kind of raucous material you never found in

Sense and Sensibility. It was a ripping yarn, to be sure, and the first great book I stumbled upon that actually seemed great.

One of the most appealing things about *Ivanhoe* was that, unlike most of the other British writers I had read, the author clearly did not occupy the moral high ground. Ferociously anti-Semitic and mad as a hatter, Scott was consciously writing bogus history that was hundreds of years out of date, fashioned in a faux-medieval style that made your bowels rumble like the loins of Saint Cuthbert. One must also grapple with Scott's hideous caricature of Isaac the Jew ("The lovers of the chase say that the hare feels more agony during the pursuit of the greyhounds than when she is struggling in their fangs. And thus it is probable that the Jews, by the very frequency of their fear on all occasions, had their minds in some degree prepared for every effort of tyranny which could be practiced upon them.") *Quick: Send a copy to Joseph Goebbels!* Isaac's stereotypical daughter Rebecca, the "Fair Flower of Palestine," whom half the characters want to rape and the other half would love to incinerate, doesn't fare much better. Scott was the first writer I ever read who was obviously morally inferior to me, and this gave me a certain comfort. I was tired of dodging the thunderbolts from Mount Parnassus; I was fed up with the idea of literature as a horsewhipping from the heavens.

More important, exposure to this out-and-out nutter enabled me to enter the world of serious literature through the back door. While everyone else was prostrating themselves before the throne of Milton, I was surreptitiously devouring Saki, Oscar Wilde, and H. G. Wells. To this very day, I have a constitutional aversion to mainstream British fiction (Muriel Spark, Iris Murdoch, Margaret Drabble, A. S.

Byatt, Anita Brookner), vastly preferring oddballs like Penelope Fitzgerald, J. G. Ballard, and Jim Crace. There is no accounting for taste; very possibly I don't have any.

As the foregoing makes clear, I have arrived at an appreciation of the British literary lions through a circuitous route. Though I majored in English in college, I never took a single course in British literature written after the eighteenth century. My heroes were Jonathan Swift, John Dryden, Alexander Pope, James Boswell, and Samuel Johnson, and to a lesser extent Henry Fielding, Laurence Sterne, and Tobias Smollett, because they were mean-spirited, funny, and irreverent, and their books didn't have any characters named Darcy.

I also came to love George Gissing's fabulously deranged *New Grub Street*. Chucked out of Owens College in 1876 for stealing, and then devoting his entire life to writing long, morose novels that weren't especially good, Gissing got all his ducks in a row only once, when he penned his classic tale about a society where literature has become a commodity like pig iron, and where writers serve, basically, as indentured slaves. The main character, Jasper Milvain, is a ruthless journalist who hopes to marry the daughter of a failed magazine editor; the object of his counterfeit affections is herself a fledgling essayist who has just inherited a substantial sum of money from the only character in the novel who is not a charter member of the literati. But the swinish Jasper (better than Balthazar or Melchior, perhaps, but still a rather strange name for a protagonist) is also putting the moves on a comely young widow whose husband died of tuberculosis or some other late-nineteenth-century malady shortly after his latest novel flopped.

Filling out this murderers' row of literary hacks is a penniless novelist whose masterpiece, *Mr. Bailey, Grocer*, tanks
at the box office. The night he finishes the novel he ventures
out for a midnight constitutional, leaving behind the only
copy of the manuscript. Naturally, the house burns down.
Luckily, he manages to rescue the manuscript and escapes
by climbing out onto the ledge and leaping to the next building. Think things are looking up? Sorry, the book gets brutal
reviews, as most novels about low-profile grocers would, and
the author, having narrowly escaped the conflagration, now
commits suicide. Obviously, Gissing had a diseased mind.
With chapters entitled "Work Without Hope," "The Last
Resource," "Rejection," "A Fruitless Meeting," "The Lonely
Man," and "Catastrophe," *New Grub Street* is easily one of
the most demented books ever written. It kept me in
stitches for weeks.

Aside from his over-the-top narrative, what I liked about
George Gissing was that he was the kind of writer you could
learn something from. To my mind, Gissing made it acceptable to go out on a limb. Writing, it should be noted, is socially
sanctioned kleptomania. When I started out in this profession,
I would sit down with my favorite authors (Graham Greene,
Henry Miller, Pliny the Younger) and record their catchiest
phrases in scores of notebooks, seeking to imitate their
rhythms and master their tricks. It didn't work, but it kept me
off the streets. Young writers learn their craft by identifying
the authors with whom they feel a certain psychic kinship and
then stealing everything that isn't nailed down. Since I personally am more sarcastic than arch, I had no time for Thackeray
or Trollope, and the stifling sincerity of George Eliot was far

from my cup of tea. But George Orwell, Jonathan Swift, and Flann O'Brien were sublime. Years later, I would come to appreciate the remarkable talents of the dreary Victorian monoliths who had caused me so much suffering as a youth. But I would do this only as a polite spectator, not as a fan.

Shakespeare posed a special problem. Like Bach, he is a one-off; he seems to have arrived, unannounced, from another planet. It is impossible to learn anything from the Bard of Avon, because, like Dante and Homer, he made his own rules, and created his own language, and only a fool would try to imitate it. Young writers can read Hemingway, Miller, and Wilde and see how they perfected a dazzling array of gimmicks. But Shakespeare didn't use any gimmicks.

The disputed authorship of Shakespeare's plays says less about Shakespeare than about those who dispute his authorship. For hundreds of years, academics have been trying to prove that Shakespeare didn't write his own plays because he didn't go to Oxford or Cambridge; he had, in the words of Ben Jonson, little Latin and less Greek. Jonson, of course, wrote raftloads of now unreadable plays. It's all a class thing; it always is in Britain. It infuriates certain people that an enigmatic rustic, a cultural entrepreneur fresh from the sticks, could have written the greatest plays in the history of mankind. But when God hands out talent, He doesn't care whom He gives it to. Giotto's father was a shepherd. George Gershwin's father worked in a shoe factory. Centuries from now, someone will surely devise a theory that the Beatles' songs were secretly penned by Sir Thomas Beecham or Henry Mancini and that V. S. Pritchett must have written "I Am the Walrus" under an assumed name because four thugs from Liverpool couldn't possibly have come up with the lyric "Semolina Pilchard, climbing up the Eiffel Tower." Shakespeare and the Beatles are an inspiration to anyone who grew up in straitened circumstances in the provinces. That's why they get up certain people's noses. To the powers-that-be, it's just not fair that Edmund Spenser didn't get to write *King Lear* or *The Merchant of Venice*. And it's simply not possible that Shakespeare did. He didn't go to the right school.

Inspirational for entirely different reasons is the masterly William Trevor. A culturally marooned Protestant who came of age in Dublin, not unlike Yeats, an Irishman who has spent a good deal of his life in Devon, Trevor has never to my knowledge written a story that is not unabashedly gloomy. His *Collected Short Stories* opens with a depressing tale about a heartless harridan who hires a bachelor to spend a weekend in a hotel with her so her husband will have grounds for divorce, and then spends the entire weekend mocking his virility. The next one features a drunken old colonel, a decrepit wretch whom everybody, including the author, despises. Next on tap is a story about an antiques dealer who is hired to reacquire a chest that a faithless man has given to his mistress; he accidentally on purpose informs the betrayed wife where the chest has been, and then demands extra payment for his efforts. Other trademark Trevor works feature the schoolboy embarrassed to introduce his mother to his friends, and the household staff who lie about the death of their employer because they do not wish to seek new positions elsewhere. One of his novels deals with a peeping Tom; another with a candy machine repairman who sells his automobile in the expectation of getting a company car from his new employer, only to find that he must drive home to his suburban semidetached in a tiny coupe with a gigantic Styrofoam fish bolted to the roof. The Trevorian cosmos is a purgatory of tubby traveling salesmen, dissolute ex-colonials, impoverished menials, lonely spinsters who fall into the clutches of con men: born losers as far as the eye can see. I once thought it would be amusing to pretend that I had come into possession of *The Kitten That Said Moo!,* a volume of humorous children's stories written in his youth that Trevor had later suppressed because he thought it would wreck his reputation as a misanthrope. But I didn't think anyone would get the joke.

I do not deny that William Trevor is a great artist, the finest short-story writer in the English language today. But that is not why I read him. I read him because, unlike Margaret Drabble, Ian McEwan, and all of the rest, he writes about people who did not go to Cambridge. His characters are not aging academics, actors, artists, politicians, and bright young things who are oh, so terribly *disappointed* that society did not turn out better; he writes about people who are merely trying to cobble together an existence, hoping against hope to pry a single honest emotion out of their cataleptic spouses. Every night, before I go to bed, I read a short story by William Trevor. I do so because I know that no matter how bad my day has been, his characters have seen worse. I'm not in it for the laughs.

AS NOTED EARLIER, WRITERS LOVE TO PRETEND THAT THE authors who first inspired them were the colossi (Dickens, Austen) or the subcolossi (Trollope, Forster). But this is nonsense. The greatest literary influence on most people's lives are books that are not very good. Danielle Steele and

Jackie Collins have had more influence on English-speaking women than Jane Austen or Anita Brookner; the defining literary experience in the average Anglo-American male's life is *The Shining* (take an ax and get rid of the entire family), *The Hunt for Red October* (Reds under the seabeds), or *Jaws* (family vacations always end badly). In my own case, I do not hesitate to say the books exerting the greatest influence on my life were *The Razor's Edge* and *Beau Geste*. Neither of these books falls into the category of "great literature." To be perfectly honest, it was not the novels themselves that changed my life forever, but the movies based upon them. In both cases, Hollywood managed to do a better job with the story than the person who wrote the novel on which the film is based. (Graham Greene once said that he preferred Carol Reed's film *The Third Man* to his own novel because the movie was "finished" in a way that the book was not.)

Though it took me decades to realize it, few books affected me more profoundly than *The Razor's Edge*. I am not alone in this conviction. Like *On the Road*, published thirteen years later, *The Razor's Edge* provides a template for anyone who ever wanted to grow up to be an angry young man and stay that way the rest of his life. The earnest saga of a dispirited World War I veteran named Laurence ("Larry") Darrell who goes off to find the meaning of life, Somerset Maugham's novel is a Cuisinart of clichés: See Larry seeking wisdom in the company of anarchist coal miners; watch Larry trek to Kathmandu to learn the arts of faith healing; oh my gosh, now Larry's hobnobbing with the raffish artists of Montmartre! I have no way of knowing whether this overwrought paean to a Roaring Twenty–something dharma bum seemed ridiculous at the time it was published, but it certainly seems ridiculous now. Today, most of us who laid off the hashish at the very last Soft Machine reunion realize that wisdom cannot be found in the mysterious Orient, much less in dank Belgian coal mines, and it has certainly long since fled Montmartre. Transformed into two ghastly movies, *The Razor's Edge* is now almost completely unreadable, a hamfisted hodgepodge of sententious banalities. But boy, did I love it when I was seventeen.

These days, it is easy to look down on *The Razor's Edge* now that every private school boy with political aspirations has spent at least one summer slumming with the working class, now that every future bond trader has communed with Shiva in the ashram, now that at least one multimillionaire center for the Boston Celtics has taken a job as a taxi driver so that he could "find himself." But I do not look down on the book. Like Larry Darrell at age twenty-one, I went off to Paris seeking the meaning of life. Like Larry, I lived in the shadow of the Boulevard Montparnasse. Like Larry, I took mindnumbing jobs with hard, defeated working-class men whose glib cynicism I fleetingly mistook for wisdom. I had no idea at the time that my entire existence was not only a cliché, but a cliché that would one day be made into a bad Bill Murray movie. All I can say in my defense is that I eventually got over it. Still, there can be no denying that a father I spent many years despising was the one who put in my hands the book that would change my life. Good thing my dad's favorite book wasn't *Crime and Punishment*. Or *The 120 Days of Sodom*.

That said, *The Razor's Edge* only holds down the no. 2 spot on the list of books that most affected me as a young man. And much as I would love to be able to single out *David Copperfield* or *Lady Chatterley's Lover* as the novel that first attracted me to the British Isles, this would not be true. The book that cast in stone the emotional infrastructure of my life was *Beau Geste,* which I read after seeing the movie. When I was nine years old, my father told me to go to bed early on Saturday night so he could wake me for an 11:30 showing of the 1939 classic. The film stars Gary Cooper, Ray Milland, and Robert Preston as English brothers who one by one flee their idyllic stately home and run off to join the French Foreign Legion after a precious jewel disappears from their mother's drawing room. (As is only to be expected, Gary Cooper was not very convincing in the role.) The movie tracks their exploits in the wilds of the Sahara, where two of the brothers fall under the dominion of the sadistic Sergeant Markoff. (Brian Donlevy, a great, though now largely forgotten Irish-American performer, was nominated for an Oscar for Best Supporting Actor.) The film features a memorable scene where one of the brothers gives his fallen sibling a Viking burial, setting his corpse ablaze with a dog nestled at his feet. The dog in question is Markoff.

It is not terribly difficult to see how this sort of gripping derring-do would enrapture a nine-year-old boy growing up in a dowdy Keystone State municipality. The kepis, the sabers, the ruthless Bedouin assaults, and most particularly the Viking funeral struck me as fiercely exotic, and caused me to fall hopelessly in love with both France and England, even though none of the action takes place in the former and very little transpires in the latter. I immediately decided that when I was old enough I would run off and join the Légion étrangère, though as luck would have it I eventually ended up running off to join the Maryknoll Missionaries, who also labored in exotic foreign lands. I never got very far in that career, either.

Years later, I found out that the French Foreign Legion of yore was composed almost exclusively of lowlifes seeking asylum from the authorities in their native lands; this diminished much of their allure, blotting their escutcheon, as it were. I also found out that they almost never won a battle; they were overwhelmed while cavorting to no good purpose in Mexico in 1863, and outgunned when the French surrendered in 1954 at Dien Bien Phu. This removed even more of their luster. Years later, when I spent many summers with my in-laws in the preposterously uninteresting town of Castelnaudary in the south of France, I got to meet real-life Legionnaires, who had set up shop there after being chucked out of Corsica for various unseemly misadventures. They were, not to put too fine a word on it, a bad lot: Yugoslavian car thieves, Iberian muscle boys, the dregs of assorted societies. These encounters annihilated the last vestiges of romance I could attach to this sordid passel of born losers.

Nevertheless, I have spent huge portions of my life in both France and England, to the exclusion of all other foreign countries, and there is no doubt that the allure of *Beau Geste* is responsible for these love affairs. When I set foot in Paris for the first time in my life, I boarded a bus from Orly Airport that traveled into Paris via the Avenue de la Légion Étrangère. Thomas Mann once said that arriving in Venice by land was like entering through the back door. For me, entering Paris by any other route than the Avenue de la Légion Étrangère would have been equally devoid of charm and symbolism. And to this very day I entertain dreams of being buried in a Viking funeral, my corpse incinerated with a dog at my feet. The dog in question would be the jackass from the *Boston Globe* who always gives my books bad reviews.

Beau Geste, published in 1924, was one of the most popular novels of all time. (It has been made into three English-language movies, one starring Leslie Nielsen and Telly Savalas, not to mention a woeful sendup entitled *The Last Remake of Beau Geste.* I do not believe this is in fact the last remake; I think we shall all live to see Mark Wahlberg, master of celluloid *recyclage* (*Planet of the Apes, The Italian Job, The Truth About Charlie*), one day straddling a bewildered camel in Sidi Bar Douania, playing the shortest French Foreign Legionnaire ever.)

The book was written by Percival Christopher Wren, a descendant of the great English architect, and an author who had clearly fallen under the spell of Robert Louis Stevenson and H. Rider Haggard as a boy. The book is recounted in a sort of official reverie by a Major Henri de Beaujolais of the Spahis, and contains all kinds of stirring lines like "How I would prick that little fellow's bubble of swank." I cannot recommend it too highly. The whole stiff-upper-lip, taking-one-for-the-team, dashing-off-to-the-tropics routine cast a spell over my malleable childhood intellect, and I have never ceased to be grateful to Mr. Wren for midwifing my seduction by both Merrie Olde England and La Belle France.

In the fullness of time, I had the opportunity to demonstrate my appreciation in a demonstrable fashion. Fifteen years earlier, I had published a story in the *Christian Science*

Monitor titled "The Fruitcakes of Albion." The story concerned the English passion for Christmas puddings, festering gobs of adamantine suet that the Brits think of as fun food, but which I view as fen food. In it, I happened to mention that my wife, Francesca, hailed from an out-of-the-way town in Gloucestershire called Stroud. But when it came time to publish the story, the copy editor, for space reasons, changed the term "out of the way" to "obscure." The story was published to universal approbation, winning me the huzzahs of the brahmins and the kudos of the cognoscenti, not to mention the undying affection of Mr. John Q. Public, whose opinion cannot be taken lightly.

But then the Stroud District Council whipped into action. Infuriated that I would dare dismiss their colorful town as "obscure," the keepers of the Cotswoldian flame fired off an angry missive, upbraiding me for willful ignorance of the cultural treasures of the region. Was I unaware that Laurie Lee, author of the imperishable classic *Cider with Rosie,* resided right up the road in Slad? (No, I knew that; I used to watch him stagger in and out of local pubs.) Had it not reached my ears that Edward II had been impaled on a red-hot poker in Berkeley Castle, just a short jaunt down the road? (Oh yes, I knew about that one.) Given these facts, how dare I call Stroud "obscure."

In my defense, I had not selected the offending term, but felt that describing Stroud as "obscure" was not entirely without factual merit, as I had never met anyone back home who had ever been to the town or expressed any desire to go there. Still, chastened and contrite, I meticulously reviewed the *District of Stroud: Official Guide* that accompanied the letter and discovered to my great amazement that Percival Wren was buried in a country churchyard in a tiny village near Minchinhampton, which sits on the crest of the gently rolling hills overlooking this much-maligned West Country burgh. A devoted obsequies buff, who never misses a chance to view the tomb of the Black Prince, or the antechamber where the irrepressible Perkin Warbeck breathed his last, I now decided that I must make a visit to the cemetery and pay my respects to this hero of my youth.

Finding the grave was not easy, in part because I spent two hours looking in the wrong graveyard. Percival Wren is buried in Amberley, but not having the guidebook close at hand I mistakenly went to nearby Avening and spent hours upon hours vainly seeking his final resting place, intermittently hectoring sextons and upbraiding passersby for their appalling indifference to my quest. In a sense, there was something reassuring about the locals' lack of interest in a writer who was clearly not in the same class as George Bernard Shaw; the English don't get excited about big things, so why should they get excited about little ones? Had Americans been running the place, there would have been a hands-on learning center where the kids could *virtually* prop up the dead Legionnaires' bodies on the walls of Fort Zinderneuf, a thirty-minute instructional video apologizing for Wren's insensitivity to people of color, and a lavish gift shop selling T-shirts reading: I CAME ALL THE WAY TO THIS T-SHIRT AND ALL I GOT WAS STROUD. Of course, you would also have to pay an admission fee to see the tomb.

That night, my brother-in-law conducted a bit of local research and unearthed the location of Wren's final resting place. The next morning, I reported to the cemetery and spent at least an hour fruitlessly seeking Wren's un-signposted grave.

Then I found it, nestled beneath a tree. The tombstone stated that he was born in 1885 and died in 1941. The site was in very bad shape, the headstone grimy, the gravestone cracked. This gave me yet another chance to reflect on the vanity of human wishes and the evanescence of fame, two of my favorite topics. Percival Wren had once been one of the best-known writers in the world. His masterpiece had been translated into innumerable languages and adapted for the screen four times. Yet here he lay, by the looks of it, forgotten and unloved. If a writer as talented and successful as Percival Wren could so quickly fall into such obscurity, what hope was there for Tom Clancy, Jackie Collins, John Grisham, James North Patterson, or Jilly Cooper? Needless to say, the fate of Ozymandias was not far from my thoughts. Nor, presumably, from Jilly Cooper's.

Bending forward, I placed a dozen yellow roses on his grave. For one to whom I owed so much, it seemed the least I could do. This was my *beau geste*. In the back of my mind, I perhaps hoped that some youngster passing through the graveyard might find his curiosity piqued by the unexpected bouquet and fall under the great man's spell. In time, this might lead to a sojourn in the Sahara or at least a trip to France. As I walked away, I whispered "thank you" to the dead novelist and promised to revisit his grave every time I came to England. In the words of George Lawrence, Esq., C.M.G., of His Majesty's Nigerian Civil Service, writing to Colonel Henri de Beaujolais, Colonel of Spahis, XIXth (African) Army Corps: "Fancy, old cabbage, after more than thirty years of devotion. I feel like a boy."

A boy who's serious about that Viking funeral.

Dog included.

5

First Prize: One Week in Wales

When I was a boy growing up in a subterranean, rat-infested drainage ditch in North Philadelphia, the only thing that kept me going was the dream that I might one day live in a glamorous suburb like Bala Cynwyd, Gladwyne, Glenolden, or Bryn Mawr. These gracious hamlets, ringing the City of Brotherly Love like a thin layer of treacle on an otherwise unsavory cake, symbolized everything I longed for in life: tradition, class, refinement, romance, a thin layer of treacle on an otherwise unsavory cake.

I never did find out why Philadelphia was surrounded by so many villages with Welsh names, but the aura of ancient, arcadian mystery that they evoked clung to me through my childhood like an asp on a sultry milkmaid's bosom. As I grew older, I became fascinated by Welsh history, steeping myself in the lore of the fourteenth-century freedom fighter Owen Glendower, the doomed miners of Rhymney, and the indomitable

Lloyd George. I devoured books by Geoffrey of Monmouth, was riveted by the descriptions of battle in the epic *The Mabinogion,* and memorized every single poem by Dylan Thomas. I was beguiled by the saga of the tiny contingent of Welsh soldiers who scared off four thousand fired-up Zulus at the Battle of Rorkes Drift (1879) merely by singing the rousing "Men of Harlech." And, of course, I collected all the films of Richard Burton.

But dreams have a way of getting away from us. I never did buy a big house in a charming Philadelphia suburb with a Welsh name; I ended up buying a small house in a so-so New York suburb with a Dutch name. But over the years, the flickering flame of Welshophilia that burned in my breast stubbornly refused to be extinguished. Whenever I visited Gloucestershire, I would be sure to make a side trip to Castell Coch, Cardiff, or Caerleon, site of the largest legionary base in Roman Britain. All the while, I continued to nurture hidden dreams of one day spending a week in Wales all by myself.

This dream finally came to fruition when I received a commission from an American men's magazine to write a story about a lawsuit in Port Meirion in which a Welsh software engineer had successfully sued his Internet service provider for using the letters *URL* without his permission. According to the plaintiff, "URL," or as it appears in Welsh, "UUURRL-LLLL," is a term that derives from the seventeenth-century Welsh word for "handy coatrack." The first known appearance of the letters *URL* in a specifically Internet context occured in 1984, when a young software technician named Rhys Davies used the letters in a self-published manual entitled

Let's Have Fun with the Commodore 64 in Welsh! Since then, the URL had become an indispensable interfacing corner-stone of the Internet. Now, the man who had invented the term wanted to be paid for it.

To prepare for my conversation with Davies, who refused to speak English, as it was "the language of the oppressor," I took a six-week course at Parliamo y Sprechen Tutti, a Man-hattan language school that teaches every language under the sun. Even though I already spoke French, could get by in Spanish and Italian, and had acquired a smattering of Greek, Portuguese, Hindi, and Yoruba over the years, I found Welsh a rather tough nut to crack. I had great difficulty pronouncing place-names like Senghenydd and Llanfihangfel-y-Pennant and could never remember whether the word *"cynefin"* referred to "the spot on a hill where a lamb was born" or "fray-ing garter belt." My teacher tried to grease the wheels by encouraging me to memorize famous Welsh limericks ("There once was a girl from Ynysybwl") but these weren't much help. Still, I stuck with it, and by the end of six weeks I felt fluent enough to converse passably. I immediately set my sights on the mountains of northern Wales.

Arriving in Cardiff after a few nights in London, I rented a car and started heading north toward Aberbowlan, where Davies lived. The instructions he'd provided were to motor straight through to Gelli-Wrgan, turn gently toward the north at Porthyrhyd, then take the first left after the second weir fifty yards outside Pontrhydfendigaid. Unfortunately, I took the third left at the third weir outside Porthyrhyd, which sent me far out of the way to Dyffryn Ardudwy, where I was forced to spend the night at the Best Western. The hotel had once been a castle in which John of Navarre's brother-in-law Robert, also of Navarre, was tortured nonstop for twenty-seven years because someone mistook him for Clarence of Narbonne. It was a dandy little establishment, and not at all expensive, but sleeping was no picnic because the Welsh nationalist lesbian party, Plaid Safficcl Cymru, was having their annual convention that weekend, and a woman in the next room kept shrieking: *"Plyth llellyth pondryrcbellog, llewellyn!"* ("Give it to me in the spot where the lamb gets born, sister!")

I rose early the next day and reached Davies's house by noon. He was a tall, gangly, forty-something man who seemed friendly, but somewhat reserved. I began peppering him with questions in Welsh, but he quickly switched to English. He graciously explained that he did not mind chatting with an American in his native tongue, but despised making this idiomatic concession to "the Saxons." I was disappointed that he found my Welsh so wanting, but perhaps not entirely surprised.

"The URL is merely the most obvious example of how the people in this country get ripped off by the *friffids* [the merchants who lurk in the tussocks]," he explained. "When the outside world thinks of Wales, they immediately conjure up images of coal miners and choirs, but did you know that the Welsh invented the reverse collateralized mortgage obligation? Did you know that the Welsh invented the semicolon, which is enormously useful in connecting mildly disparate thoughts? Did you know that chewing gum was invented by a Welshman named Wwwrriggley, who sold the recipe—for a widow's pittance—to an American with a similar name?"

Of these things I was not aware, though other examples of cultural vandalism and outright theft had already reached my ears. I knew, for example, that the popular Black Russian beverage had, until 1956, been known as the Black Welshman, and that Welsh Fly, Welsh Omelets, and Welsh Waffles antedated the Spanish and Belgian varieties by many centuries. I had also read in Travis Godwin's book *My Lantern Still Burns in the Valley, But It's Going Out Fast* that sixteenth-century Welsh seamstresses had invented hot pants as a mechanism for stemming the plummeting reproductive rate, and that the Welsh had invented photosynthesis, solar power, the gilt-edged RSVP invitation, genome research, wah-wah pedals, liner notes, gelato, and the adult diaper.

"Walt Disney spent two years as a young man working as a stevedore in Port Meirion, and that's where he got the idea for theme parks," Davies continued. "Géricault lifted *The Raft of the Medusa* whole cloth from Gwyn Tremorgan's *Now, Men of Caerphilly, Swim for It!* Tennessee Williams's *Cat on a Hot Tin Roof* was originally set in Caermarthen. The theme that introduces the third movement of Couperin's *Airs Gracieux et Etincelants* is a note-for-note repackaging of an old miners' ditty called 'When the Moon Comes over Glamorgan, I'll Already Be in Abershyll.' Spanish, regardless of what the Texas Tornados may claim, is not 'the loving tongue'; it is Welsh. *Flashdance* was once known as *Fflllashhdantse*; *Thelma & Louise* was originally called *The Thrilling Adventures of Gwynneth and Rhonda.* The plots of both *Donnie Brasco* and *La Dolce Vita* are derived from the sixth-century Welsh epic *How Gog Smote the Tryffyds.* I think you get my general drift."

What particularly infuriated Davies was the reluctance of so many famous people of Welsh ancestry to proclaim their true ethnic identity.

"You can see just by looking at him that Francis Ford Coppola is Welsh," the software engineer, inventor, historian, and cultural activist seethed. "Bette Midler has the prominent buttocks that are typical of middle-aged Welsh women, yet she persists in pretending to be Jewish. Jerry Lewis is Welsh, as is Keanu Reeves. Jim Morrison felt so guilty about denying his Welshness that he drank himself to death. As long as famous people continue to repudiate their true ethnic roots, it will be that much more difficult for all of us."

As I was leaving that day, Davies handed me a copy of a recently published book called *The Gifts of the Welsh: How One Tiny Nation Gave Civilization Everything and Got Nothing in Return Except the Euro.* I stayed up all night reading it from cover to cover. It was electrifying stuff, a real eye-opener. Cole Porter was Welsh. Two of the figures in Picasso's *Les Demoiselles d'Avignon* were chambermaids from Porthmadog. Sauerkraut is a Welsh invention, as are muffler repair, postcards, variable annuities, and frankincense. Debit cards were invented by the Welsh, not to mention patterned pajamas and kitty litter; the term "No tickee, no laundry" was coined by a Swansea cleaning lady of mixed Chinese and Welsh ancestry; and the phrase "There'll be tears before bedtime" was first used by a Welsh henchman of Henry I who had been sent to Paergyrydd Castle to blind Henry's brother Robert because Henry himself was incapacitated by shingles. *Casablanca* originally centered on Italian spies operating in prewar Wales, but Samuel Goldwyn, though himself Welsh, did not think a movie called *It Happened in Machynlleth* would sell and had the locale shifted to exotic Morocco.

That night, I thought back to my childhood in Philadelphia, when names like Bala Cynwyd and Lower Merion had spawned those many-splendored dreams. I was happy that I had come to Wales, and prepared to do whatever I could to get the message out about the ruthless pillaging of Welsh culture. So the next time you hear Mendelssohn's *Italian Symphony*, remember that it was originally called *The Welsh Symphony*. The next time you read Thomas Mann, bear in mind that the German Nobelist's greatest novella was originally entitled *Death in Aberystwyth*. And the next time you look at those magnificent water lilies by a colossus you had always assumed to be French, keep in mind, Clydd Mynett was born in Llenfyllen.

6

Take It to Ye Olde Limit
One More Time

When I first read Lewis Carroll's *Alice in Wonderland* in my teens, I interpreted it as a chimerical fantasy about an innocent young girl who disappears down a rabbit hole and enters a phantasmagoric society populated by lunatics. Not until I married an Englishwoman and started visiting Old Blighty did I realize that Carroll was merely describing Britain. After a quarter century of crisscrossing this deceptively bizarre country, I can say, without fear of being contradicted, that *Alice in Wonderland* is a brutally realistic novel that faithfully describes Britain as she is, as she was, as she always will be. Britain is a strange, emotionally unhinged society where aberrant behavior is the norm, and as such *Alice in Wonderland* is as scrupulously attentive to factual detail as Zola's *Germinal,* Dreiser's *An American Tragedy,* or Dostoyevsky's *The Brothers Karamazov.* In British society, where weirdness lurks in every corner, the unsuspecting tourist may find himself vanishing down not one but any number of rabbit holes every day. The Britain of Dickens and Hardy has come and gone; the Britain of Lewis Carroll is as plain as the nose on your face. If you're looking for misfits, crackpots, and loonies, you've come to the right place.

Item: One evening I had drinks with a journalist who set out to write a story about nightclub bouncers and became so enamored of the occupation that he started working as a bouncer himself. When I queried him about recurrent reports that Soho bouncers were guilty of pummeling patrons into submission—sometimes in full view of the ubiquitous security cameras that have ushered Britain into the post-Orwellian nightmare—he replied that the bouncers were rarely at fault, that they were merely "professionals" doing their jobs. No one back where I come from would ever describe a bouncer as a "professional"; a professional is a person with vast amounts of training and expertise who is expected to adhere to a strict code of ethics and can be sued if he does not. A bouncer is a person with a gigantic steak tartare for a face who has never read Bossuet's *Discours sur l'histoire universelle.* This is really the only way to tell the occupations apart. Moreover, no one back where I come from would ever switch from being a journalist to being a bouncer. They do it the other way around and go to work for *Maxim.*

Item: At an Oxford reenactment industry trade show where canny craftsmen representing companies with names like Dressed to Kill hawk Plantagenet-style cuirasses, Crecy Era longbows, discount mead, and flouncy camp-follower gowns just perfect for brisk autumn evenings in Agincourt, a reenactment specialist who had "monitored" more than one hundred mock battles to guarantee their authenticity candidly informed me that the sight of a woman decked out in medieval garb struck him as quite fetching. I told him I was going to stick with maids, nurses, and cheerleaders.

Item: In preparation for a BBC television appearance, I had ventured into the Institute of Contemporary Art to see a video installation featuring two Dutch anorexics who moped, pouted, and periodically fed each other peanuts. The installation had provoked considerable outrage among politicians and pundits, who felt that it was glorifying anorexia. I saw the video and thought it was glorifying peanuts. As in the United States, British politicians only discuss art to deplore it, acting as if they spent all their free time gaping at Holbein's portrait of Thomas More or Paul Delaroche's *The Execution of Lady Jane Grey,* when the closest they ever get to an art museum is the postcard rack in the Majorca surf shop. I happened to see the anorexics in question in the museum café; they appeared to be sharing a salad. I'd heard of young people visiting Europe on peanuts, but these gals were pushing it. Kurt Vonnegut once said that modern art was a conspiracy between artists and rich people to make everyone else feel stupid, but this pair merely made me feel hungry. I had a burger with extra fries.

As I was exiting the museum, the receptionist at the information desk asked if I was Joe Queenan. As usual, I was. She had read several of my books and seen me on television; she was "a big fan." The phrase "big fan" always gives me the willies; the speaker invariably wants a fiver or David Letterman's home number. But no, the woman asked if I would be taking in a football match during my trip. I said I would be.

She proudly announced that she was an Arsenal season ticket holder and invited me to a late-season game against the team's despised crosstown rivals, the Tottenham Hotspurs. I took her up on it, even though I secretly feared that I would be set upon and beaten by thugs, infuriated that I had written a less than enthusiastic *New York Times* review of Nick Hornby's latest novel. Arsenal won 2–1 on a late penalty kick by someone who definitely was not English. You could not possibly visit an American museum hosting a video exhibition of anorexic Netherlands nut-nibblers and be offered tickets to a football game; everyone in the American art world loathes professional sport. Things like this only happen in Britain.

Item: In North Woodchester, Gloucestershire, there is an ancient Roman mosaic floor that used to be opened to the public once every ten years, but unfortunately I had never made it to an unveiling. On my most recent trip to the Cotswolds, I found out that the floor had now been sealed over *in aeternum*. Dismayed, a group of local artisans spent more than a year constructing a replica of the historical curiosity, all at their own expense. The resulting mosaic measures fourteen square meters, contains 1.6 million tiles, weighs 3.5 tons, and is the largest such object north of the Alps. At the end of their labors they were informed by the draconian Stroud District Council that there was no public space to display the impressive tile-laden doppelgänger, so they might as well stuff it up in the attic until a bit of exhibition space opened up the third Tuesday after Armageddon. Meanwhile, right down the road in South Woodchester, whose name appears in William the Conqueror's *Domesday Book,* a group of inept Roman Empire reenactors catapulted wooden missiles into the air and smashed up somebody's tiled roof.

Item: My brother-in-law, an avid supporter of amateur rugby, continues to write acerbic, fulminating letters to the local newspaper even though he stopped going to the Gloucester club's games several years ago when the squad turned professional. The team was mesmerizingly horrible in the waning years of its amateur status, but has since vaulted to the very top of the sport. Tony, a man of principle, does not care; he longs for a simpler, more innocent time, when rugby teams were composed entirely of feisty local lads who competed for free, and usually played like it. As a result, he travels 130 miles every other Saturday to watch a resolute amateur squad knock heads in Devon. It is composed of old men who used to be mediocre and young men who, if they really work at it, can one day be so-so. He also roots for the Scots, the Irish, and even the Welsh when they face off against the English national team; the English in 2003 achieved the nearly unimaginable feat of defeating both the French and the Australians—on their own pitch in New South Wales—to win the World Cup. The entire nation exploded in paroxysms of joy; Tony was disconsolate. Most Americans turn to *Fawlty Towers* or *Masterpiece Theater* to study the classic English eccentric in his native habitat. But I didn't have to go looking for eccentricity; I married into it.

Item: Arriving at London's Groucho Club, I once handed my luggage to a porter who quite simply could not find his way to my room. The combination club-hotel had recently annexed a building next door, and was admittedly a bit of a maze, but after five minutes of frantically leading me up and down stairs, through archways, and down corridors, the man finally had to admit that he was beaten and retreated downstairs to summon the concierge. The concierge, armed with a detailed floor plan, finally cracked the mystery.

I am still waiting for my luggage.

Item: I was strolling through Regent's Park one morning on the way to meet a dear friend, but first decided to pop into the men's room. Entering, I spotted a toilet attendant in a tiny office who appeared to be buried in paperwork. I asked him for directions to Queen Mary's Gardens, because my friend's cryptic directions ("If you imagine that the garden is a lollypop, I will be standing at the point where the stem meets the taffy") had proven confusing. But the man was too busy to talk, as he was buried in paperwork. This left me with two questions that will torment me until my dying day.

1. Isn't it a bit hard to do paperwork with all those horrible smells engulfing you?
2. What kind of paperwork do toilet attendants do?

Item: While strolling through Hyde Park one morning, I happened upon a fussy old woman who was giving a thirtyish man some badly needed lessons in dog training.

"You have to show them who's in charge; otherwise you're just lost," she explained. "For example, when it's time to go home, you don't want to tug at their collars and force them to obey; you have to make your wishes clear through the tone of your voice. You have to say 'BYE-EE, BYE-EE' in a loud voice. And then they know it's time to come. Now you try it."

The young man tethered at the far end of a Jack Russell

was wearing a prim blue suit with a snappy tie, and did not seem dressed for the occasion. He hesitated to follow her instructions.

"Go on," she insisted. "Say BYE-EE, BYE-EE."

"Bye-ee, bye-ee," he croaked, halfheartedly.

"No, say BYE-EE, BYE-EE," she hectored him.

"Bye-ee, bye-ee," he repeated without enthusiasm or authority, seemingly quite embarrassed by the whole situation. Just then, a mammoth black hound who looked like he might have been with Hereward the Wake when he made his last stand at Ely in the eleventh century thundered across the lawn and leaped at the terrier, taking a nice bite out of his diminutive hide. The beleaguered pooch leaped into his owner's arms, smearing fresh mud all over his jacket, and the woman promptly disappeared. The owner of the hound, a middle-aged man decked out in tweed, corduroy, and a Greek fisherman's cap—the traditional Ragged-Trousered Philanthropist getup—rushed over, patted the frightened little victim, and assured the owner that no permanent harm had been done. But could he quit while he was behind? He could not.

"He doesn't care much for Jack Russells," he apprised the victim's owner. Then, turning to me, he confided in a conspiratorial tone, "They abused him as a pup."

The hound was the size of a Ford Escort, making it hard to imagine all but the most ferocious Jack Russell taking him on, even as a callow youth. As man and beast scurried off, I asked the owner of the still petrified doggy why the obedience trainer had vanished so abruptly just when things got a bit dicey.

"I never saw her before in my life," he said, not for a second betraying any sense that these recent events were even slightly out of the ordinary. "Actually, it's not even my dog. My boss asked me to take him for a walk."

I MENTION THESE INCIDENTS, WHICH BY NO MEANS HAVE exhausted the shelves of my anecdotal larder, purely to illustrate that unconventional attitudes and behavior are not something one need actively seek in Britain; weirdness has its own way of finding you. Indeed, I have begun to conceive of this great, highly mythologized nation as one vast eccentricity factory where oddities lurk behind every door, just as America is one vast building site where grotesque architectural plans lurk behind every door.

One night, I was returning home from seeing Vanessa Redgrave in an undernourished production of *Lady Windermere's Fan*. Gliding past the bus stop catty-corner to Victoria Station, the kind of venerable, all-purpose public transportation hub that does not exist in the United States, I happened to notice a sign for a service called the Oxford Tube. The Tube, closer scrutiny revealed, operated twenty-four hours a day, with buses leaving London every twelve minutes during peak hours, and with service at twenty past the hour straight through the night. I could not imagine even the most indefatigable tourist feeling an obligation to visit the Ashmolean in the middle of the night. My curiosity piqued, I decided to take a short nap and then grab the 4:20 A.M. bus. I was desperate to learn what type of insatiable, night-owl culture vulture could possibly be taking a bus to Oxford in that eerie interlude between the witching hour and rosy-fingered dawn.

As things turned out, the double-decker was filled with stinking drunks. Confiscating the beer cans at the door, the driver, a tough but cheerful Anglo-Indian who sounded like a Punjab Michael Caine, explained that while pubs throughout England closed at midnight, private London clubs stayed open all night, allowing desperate rustics to hop on a bus to the capital and get blasted. I now had the answer to my question, but was already headed for Oxford at a quarter to five in the morning, uncertain what I would do when I arrived.

What I did was nothing. There isn't anything to do in Oxford, or any other small, provincial English town, at six o'clock in the morning; there's not that much to do at six in the evening. So I walked around, trying to stay warm, periodically ducking into cafés and coffee bars as the enchanting municipality gradually came to life. When the bells tolled ten, I decided to head over to the Ashmolean Museum to see William Holman Hunt's *A Converted British Family Sheltering a Christian Missionary,* as any serious connoisseur of ridiculous paintings would. The Ashmolean is just a short jaunt from the Bath Place Hotel where Richard Burton and Liz Taylor used to have their famous assignations during the Swinging Sixties, and where I had a somewhat less spectacular assignation with my wife in 1999. The Bath Place Hotel is worthy of note, in that it tilts. You cannot put your drink down anywhere in the room because the building lists slightly to the right. My wife and I had our drinks standing up. As God is my witness.

I was headed nowhere in particular when I happened to pass the Bate Collection of Musical Instruments, a pocket-sized museum that is huddled in a corner not far from Christ Church. Stepping in, I was immediately greeted by a gregarious young woman in a subdued green dress that may have been filched from Anne Hathaway's wardrobe. I nodded, said hello, then wandered about a bit, eyeing the princely clavichords and regal pianos.

"You can play any of the harpsichords except for that one over there," she informed me. "We believe that one may have belonged to Handel."

"I don't really like the harpsichord," I replied, recalling many dismal evenings in drafty French churches suffering through Vivaldi and Telemann while a young student. In France, there is a law dating from the time of Louis XV stipulating that at any given hour of the day or night, someone, somewhere within the nation's borders must be performing *The Four Seasons*. Otherwise, the crops will fail. I had always dismissed Vivaldi's work as slapdash piffle—music for the king's supper—and didn't rate Telemann or Scarlatti, the latter born the same year as Bach, much higher. And contrary to what musical preservationists believe, if Bach were alive today, there is no way he would choose to have his music performed on the harpsichord, as it is an unbelievably annoying instrument, the baroque equivalent of the accordion.

"You only say that because the modern harpsichord is usually tuned to the wrong pitch," said the woman in the ecstatically sober dress. She had the charming name of Hélène La Rue, but was not French, or at least took pains not to act like it. She then launched into a lengthy explanation of the history of harpsichord tuning, which I found absolutely fascinating, even though I could not understand any of it. She also pointed out that keys had different meanings and that musicians often preferred some to others; I vaguely remembered Keith Richards and Bruce Springsteen complaining that it was difficult to play with Chuck Berry because he always switched to weird keys like B-flat in the middle of a song, for no other reason than to enrage people who were richer than he. At the conclusion of her tidy peroration she went over to the staircase, looked heavenward, and spoke to someone I could not see.

"Chris, could you come down and play for a few minutes?" she asked. A fortyish man now descended the stairs, seated himself at Handel's putative harpsichord, and began to play *The Goldberg Variations*. Peachy! As a child, I had dreamed that my life would eventually take this shape, that I would wander in off the streets of a strange city on a frigid March morning and find myself in a museum of rare musical instruments where I would be personally serenaded on George Frideric Handel's harpsichord to the strains of Johann Sebastian Bach's exalted keyboard music. But things like that never happened in the United States because the country had not been around long enough to create the infrastructure of zaniness that makes England such a delight. Also, Philadelphia musicians are unionized.

As Chris worked his way through an exquisite rendering of Bach's chef d'oeuvre, my hostess took me on a brief tour of the museum. She proudly pointed out one of Adolphe Sax's original saxophones and explained that one reason the instrument failed to gain immediate popularity was stout resistance from French manufacturers of brass instruments. This I had not known. Desperate to prove that I was not a complete philistine, I served up a few tidbits regarding attempts by Japanese collectors to corner the market on vintage guitars, even though guitars do not have a long shelf life and will become useless in about one hundred years. We also discussed Hector Berlioz's disastrous marriage to the English actress Harriet Smithson, the effect of Robert Schumann's insanity on his career as a composer (it didn't help), why Paul Hindemith's *Symphonic Metamorphoses on Themes of Carl Maria von Weber* was not better known, and Gustav Holtst's sideline career as an inventor of musical instruments. (He was English, not German, and lived in Cheltenham, home of the Rolling Stones' Brian Jones.) At the end, she graciously noted that unforeseen little tête-à-têtes like this "warmed the cockles of the curatorial heart."

Meanwhile, Chris hammered away on the old 88s. Or 66s. After a long chat, I asked Miss La Rue if she could direct me to the men's room. She provided detailed directions, and explained that the group of scholarly types I might encounter along the way were visiting musicians in town for a convention. I slipped past her and plowed straight into a room filled with people clutching what appeared to be cellos. But they were not cellists; they were members of the British Viola da Gamba Society, which had converged on Oxford for their annual get-together. Many of the ancient or faux-ancient (some were of recent vintage) instruments were quite ornate; several had their tops carved in the shape of human heads.

"Is that Joseph Stalin?" I asked a man who was clutching a particularly striking instrument.

"No, it's George the Fifth," he replied, not at all indig-

nantly. I wasn't so sure. It looked to me like some unscrupu-
lous Soviet black marketeers may have unloaded a bunch of
dodgy Stalin-era viola da gambas on Pommy huckleberries
back in the mid-fifties when the Old Soviet Iron Man went
down for the count. But I said nothing at the time.

I spent the rest of the day immersed in the arcane world of
British music. I gabbed with the viola da gamba ensemble. I
resumed my chitchat with Miss La Rue. Then I repaired to a
local pub where Ian Cole, the recently purged curator of the
Oxford Museum of Modern Art, regaled me with stories
about meeting Jerry Lee Lewis in a club on the Yorkshire
moors called La Dolce Vita when he was still just a boy.
United by a common passion for pop culture, we traded stories back and forth; I told him about meeting Elvis Costello at
a hotel pool in Los Angeles, where he informed me that Franz
Liszt's last student had only recently died; my companion
diverted me with an account of Pete Townsend's surprise visit
to Oxford, insisting that the rock star was "a prince of a man,"
a statement I had some trouble accepting, as Townsend had
founded the Who. Mind you, I had never met Cole before; I
had been given his number by a London friend. It was one of
the high points of my entire visit to Britain. The Chinese say
that one of life's greatest pleasures is to meet a countryman in
a strange land, but I much prefer meeting a stranger in a
strange land. Especially if he's strange. Then I went over to
the Holywell Music Room where a group of Japanese and
German professionals traveling under an assumed name
(Charivari Agréable) showed the amateur viola da gambistas
how it was really done. All this because I'd clambered onto a
bus in Victoria in the middle of the night.

■ ■ ■

MY IMPROMPTU TRIP TO OXFORD REAFFIRMED WHAT I HAD long found to be the case in Britain: If you merely pushed in a door, any door, an entirely unexpected experience would be waiting on the other side. But it also supplied abundant evidence of the British passion for musical styles that had long gone out of vogue. This passion was much in evidence when I attended a concert at St. John's Smith Square a few nights later. The concert in question featured the Academy of Ancient Music under the baton of its founder, Christopher Hogwood. Hogwood and his ensemble have a fetishistic obsession with performing baroque, rococo, and classical compositions on the instruments that were in use at the time. They do a great deal of research into tempos and speeds, and frantically labor to recapture a past that is long gone and may have never existed. This is all well and good, but I am sure that if Handel, Bach, and Mozart were alive today they would tell Hogwood and the gang to ditch the *cors de chase* and viola da gambas and take up the instruments in common use today. The piano was basically invented because Beethoven kept breaking the delicate, rickety pianofortes that were the only instruments available to him at the time. When Liszt finished a concert, the stage looked like a keyboard cemetery. Not *all* progress is bad.

The soloist at the performance was a pianist named Robert Levin. He was a bit of a show-off; he got up my nose. (There is no American equivalent for the expression "He got up my nose"—it dwells in that shadowy zone between "He rubbed me the wrong way" and "He really pissed me off"—but up my

nose he got.) After a passable rendition of Mozart's Piano
Concerto no. 24, he invited members of the audience to write
down a series of notes on little slips of paper, on which he
then played variations in the style of Beethoven, Stravinsky,
and Mozart. During the intermission, I asked if he could also
knock off an impromptu Webern or Schoenberg miniature.
Yes, he replied, but why bother? All in all, Levin had inserted
a nice parlor trick into his act, but I had seen John Tesh, a
blow-dried American television presenter turned schlocky
bandleader, resort to a similar stunt at Carnegie Hall a few
years earlier. I dislike schmaltzy classical musicians who pan-
der to the masses; you never see Maurizio Pollini or the
Olympian Sir Colin Davis pulling this nonsense. It's coy; it's
condescending; it's Lang Langism at its worst. The concert
concluded with a performance of Mozart's Concert Rondo in
D Major for Piano, which was serviceable in the way these
things tend to be, but certainly no more. Throughout the evening, I had the distinct impression that the musicians viewed
themselves primarily as keepers of a flickering flame, custodians of a fading dream. There was something fussy about the
whole business; they were not so much performers as reenactment specialists.

A few nights later, I went to a small club in Shoreditch to
see a band called the Rapiers. Shoreditch is one of those hot
up-and-coming areas in East London that hip young people
adore because it is grubby and slightly dangerous and has not
yet been discovered by anyone but them, though to the naked
eye it seems merely crummy. People who grew up in crummy
neighborhoods are impervious to the allure of run-down areas,
just as people who grew up in the suburbs are blind to the

charms of the suburbs. In fact, the suburbs have no charm, because all the interesting young people have fled to the cities where they live in crummy, up-and-coming neighborhoods. That makes these neighborhoods more exciting. It doesn't make them any less crummy.

The Rapiers are a group of three middle-aged men (with a younger bass player) who play the music that was popular in the very early 1960s before the Beatles and the Stones blasted it into obsolescence. Decked out in natty suits with calf-high boots and pencil-tin neckties, the Rapiers perform perfect, note-for-note renditions of such Beat Era classics as "Apache," "Telstar," "Tequila," and "Wipe Out." They meticulously reenact all the classic steps of the Shadows and the Ventures and others of their ilk, but rarely play anything recorded after 1963. Their records include *Return of the Rapiers* and *Los Rapiers;* needless to say they are available in a vinyl format. They put out an ebullient but incorrectly punctuated newsletter (*The Rapiers News*) written in breathless early-sixties style in which they scampishly refer to themselves as "the lads." In it, they lift their fans' spirits with the news that their latest LP will not only include a cut by Mike Sheridan and the Nightriders, but a long-forgotten Shane Fenton and the Fentones number that they unearthed on a "rare Scopitone jukebox video." The lads sometimes appear in vests. Their leader, Colin V. Pryce-Jones, is quite a tall man, with pusillanimous Clark Kent glasses and a jubilant, crackling guitar style. If his remarkable wig were as persuasive as his solos, he would be in very fine fettle indeed.

The mood in the room the night of the concert occupied the strange no-man's-land between affection (a good emotion) and irony (a bad one): The band, true believers all, seemed to genuinely adore the music they were performing, and acted as if they were evoking a bygone Classical Age; the audience seemed to be enjoying the show with a kind of nudge-nudge, wink-wink playfulness. The crowd included quite a few neo–Carnaby Mods whose attire was doubly anachronistic: utterly retro by today's standards, but far too hip for the era being evoked. They were like fresh-faced African-American hipsters donning pimp clothes for a latter-day Martha and the Vandellas reunion: They were off by about five years.

The bouncer at the door, a jumbo-sized black man, seemed to find the cheerfully corny show highly engaging; one of the musicians later told me that bouncers must be present whenever music is played in clubs, and the muscle man was relieved to be working a show where no metal detectors were required. Still, I hate it when black people get to see white people at their most uncompromisingly silly; I am always embarrassed when the black store clerk sneers at my stack of Christmas gifts (*Oklahoma!*; *Come Fly with Me*; *Viva, Las Vegas!*) and I have to explain: "I'm sorry, I'm white."

Late in the evening, Pryce-Jones paid a backhanded tribute to George Harrison, a wonderful man who had recently died a horrible death. Unlike my parents, who got to see Frank Sinatra, Duke Ellington, Louis Armstrong, Artie Shaw, Tony Bennett, Rosemary Clooney, Ella Fitzgerald, Benny Goodman, and Bing Crosby live to ripe old ages, baby boomers will spend their declining years in a world prematurely stripped of John Lennon, George Harrison, Elvis Presley, Brian Jones, and Roy Orbison, not to mention Jim

Morrison, Janis Joplin, Jimi Hendrix, and the guy from Thin Lizzy. I view this as both unfair and unhealthy; when Keith Richards goes, I'm going with him.

Anyway, George. Capriciously sniping that he'd never cared much for the Beatles (which was a bit like saying that Jack the Ripper, who'd operated nearby, lacked panache), Pryce-Jones launched into a żippy rendition of "Roll Over, Beethoven," on which George used to sing the lead vocal with the Beatles. The band did a smashing job; in the parlance of the jejune, they kicked it. At this moment, I was struck by the amazing similarities between Pryce-Jones and Hogwood. Both men earnestly believed that a golden age of music had once existed, but had now passed. Both men believed that music should be faithfully reproduced on period instruments, with strict attention to historical detail. Both men were desperately attempting to prevent a now-flickering flame from expiring forever. What was yet more fascinating was this: While most music lovers are nostalgic for a glittering bygone era, the Rapiers and the Academy of Ancient Music were nostalgic for an age that actually preceded the era everyone else was nostalgic for. Most aging hipsters hark back to the Golden Age of the Stones and the Kinks; these outfits pined for the Bronze Age of Dick Dale and Link Wray. The Rapiers were, in their own quaint way, simply another Academy of Ancient Music. The only real difference was that Christopher Hogwood's ensemble never played surf music. And the Rapiers had no Gibsons da Gamba.

Again and again throughout my travels I would be exposed to this peculiar genre of pop antiquarianism. One night in York I attended a concert given by the Paul Judge Duo. Judge

himself was a skilled blues stylist identified in the program as
"former slide columnist" for *Guitarist Magazine*. Since then,
his journalism career had perhaps slid. Fiercely Caucasian,
and a bit on the scholarly side, Judge would introduce songs
by Panama Red and Elmore James with a studiousness that
suggested he might have been talking about Alessandro
Stradella's *Exsultate, Jubilate*. Then he would perform the
songs in a deliberate, respectful, pedantic fashion that lacked
the grit and angst and salaciousness that great blues music
requires. Judge was certainly a well-meaning performer, and a
gifted slide guitarist. But, unlike Son House and Howlin'
Wolf, he sipped orange juice between songs. The overall
effect was like watching Pierce Brosnan trying to impersonate
Blind Lemon Jefferson. Or vice versa. The great blues masters played steel guitar; Paul Judge played Remington Steele
guitar.

YET BY FAR MY STRANGEST AND MOST MEMORABLE EXPERI-
ence in musical archivism took place in a tiny auditorium in
Stroud. One afternoon, as I was bouncing past the Subscription Rooms, a combination tourist information office and
concert hall, I spied a flyer for a rock band called Talon.
Talon, I quickly learned, was a West Country Eagles tribute
band. When I was conducting the research for my book
Red Lobster, White Trash, and the Blue Lagoon, I spent a year
trying to find anything anywhere in any art form that was
actually worse than *Cats*. Reassuringly, it did not exist and, to
the best of my knowledge, it still does not. But during this
hegira from sanity, I fleetingly became a connoisseur of the

obviously revolting: *Riverdance;* Kenny G, Billy Joel, especially in his classical phase. Now that I was in England, my more cynical friends encouraged me to adopt a similar approach: spending a week at Butlin's, gambling in Blackpool, visiting Madame Tussaud's, reading lots of Jilly Cooper novels. Generally, I had resisted such malignant overtures, no longer having the stomach for the nether regions of popular culture. But for Talon, I would make an exception.

I rushed back to my in-laws' house, breathless with excitement, eager to line up recruits for my Friday night expedition. The response was not encouraging. No one was interested in the Eagles, much less an English Eagles tribute band. Years earlier, my brother-in-law had seen the Beatles at the Subscription Rooms, just before the band exploded. He didn't need any stinking tribute bands.

I diligently explained that this was not the point. The very notion of attending an Eagles tribute concert in a small hamlet in the bosom of the Cotswolds was imbued with too much irony to be ignored. Yes, irony is a bad emotion, but I am a bad human being. My brother-in-law, by contrast, does not have an ironic bone in his body, which is one reason I like him. Other friends found my proposition equally easy to rebuff. The Eagles were an absurdly lightweight pop band who had once, without any provocation, recorded a song cowritten by Ronald Reagan's stepdaughter. Attending a concert given by a bunch of English rustic wannabes was not their idea of a rewarding Friday night. They'd rather stay at home playing cribbage. Five or six cards; didn't matter to them.

I was not to be put off. So Friday night I lined up front and center, the first person to pass through the Subscription

Rooms' doors. I expected no more than a handful of audience members, but I was stunned to find a crowd of more than two hundred. And not just people my age. There were hippies in motorcycle jackets with Methuselahan ponytails, to be sure, and several women in Hell Freezes Over Tour bomber jackets, but there were also young girls, young men, small children, and a number of people who were obviously well into their seventies. One man was actually carrying a cane.

If I was expecting a two-bit, half-assed ensemble like those forlorn tribute bands that turn up in local American saloons everywhere, I was in for a surprise. The stage was littered with fourteen guitars, a mandolin, keyboards, congas, and even a pedal steel guitar. Talon was no slipshod, fly-by-night outfit; had they not recently played the Theatr Elli in Llanelli and the Cheese & Grain in Frome? The concert was a bit late in getting started, as the lead guitarist got stuck in traffic, but once the familiar strains of "Hotel California" pierced the March stillness, it was crisp, crackling professionalism all the way. Although I had always found the Eagles just a tad hooty, even a jaundiced old turnip like me had to be impressed by the musicianship on display that night. Indeed, as the band ripped through the first three numbers, it was almost possible to close your eyes and imagine that it was really Don Henley, Glenn Frey, Joe Walsh, and the other two guys from the Eagles up there on stage. "Hotel California" was *tasty*! "Tequila Sunrise" was *smoking*! "Lyin' Eyes" kicked the proverbial *ass*! And as the band worked their way through the set list, more and more audience members wandered into the aisle and began to swivel and sway. Some of them looked like they may have been on hand when the Beatles headed that memorable double bill with the Rebel Rousers in 1963. Some danced to remember. Some danced to forget.

I do not, and did not, dance.

The illusion that the real-life Eagles were on stage was abruptly shattered when Chris Lloyd, the lead singer, opened his mouth and implored the audience to "Give it up for Conrad Carpenter of Herefordshire." Lloyd did not sound like he was from Southern California. He didn't even sound like he was from southern Herefordshire. A typical British front man, he regaled the audience with a string of slightly risqué jokes and abysmal puns that further vitiated the illusion that one was caught in the epicenter of the Henleyan maelstrom. With his hail-fellow-well-met demeanor, he reminded me of innumerable British music hall performers, mixing a kind of Morecambe-and-Wise silliness with standard-issue Benny Hill ribaldry.

Afterward, I found out that Talon was only one of many Eagles tribute bands that crisscrossed Eagles-adultating Albion—and even Norway—serenading entertainment-challenged rustics in provincial towns like Hornchurch and Abergavenny. There were Illegal Eagles—whose poster screamed "Attitude! Attitude!"—and a band called Flock of Eagles, and at least two others. There were also innumerable Stones, Beatles, Queen, and Led Zeppelin tribute bands, not to mention the dreaded Abba impersonators Björn Again. Seemingly, the members of Talon converged on each venue from different towns in the West Country; their offices were in Coventry, another city the Germans tried to blow up in the war. (The firebombing of Dresden in 1945 is widely thought to be payback for the destruction of Coventry Cathedral in 1940. It is not clear how this compensatory bombardment has affected the Kraftwerk tribute band industry.)

After the concert, I visited the lads backstage. It soon became apparent that they were talented, working musicians who had never really made it big, and had settled on this sideline career as a way to pay the bills. In fact, they had considered paying tribute to several other bands before deciding on the Eagles. It wasn't even that clear how much they liked the Eagles. But none of them liked punk. I never did find out why people in this country were so taken with the Eagles, but it obviously did not seem anywhere near as strange to them as it did to me. Nothing ever does.

A FEW WEEKS LATER, I ARRIVED IN GLASGOW AT SUNDOWN and walked into the Royal Concert Hall. I told the ticket clerk that if there was a concert on tap that evening, I would like one seat, unless the performer in question was Ravi Shankar. The clerk informed me that Georgie Fame and the Blue Flames were scheduled to give a concert with the Animals (minus Eric Burdon and Alan Price, which was sort of like the Apaches sans Geronimo), Zoot Money, and the Rebel Rousers, who had played with the Beatles in the Stroud Subscription Rooms almost forty years earlier. I grabbed my ticket.

The concert would prove to be a bittersweet experience. There were fewer people at the concert than at the Talon event; a friend later explained that the Scottish national soccer team was playing the French that evening, so everyone was at home watching the telly. The Scots got hammered, 6–0, as they usually got hammered, 6–0. (Later that week, their rugby team got thumped even worse.) This was a poor excuse for shunning one of the greatest living keyboardists and vocalists. Georgie Fame had backed Sonny Boy Williamson and Howlin' Wolf on their first trip to England. He had played with everyone from Van Morrison to John Lee Hooker, and had played keyboards with Bill Wyman's Rhythm Kings at Town Hall in New York City in November 2002, without question one of the most joyous concerts I ever attended. Though perhaps not a god himself, he had touched the raiment of the gods. Fame put on a wonderful show, acting as if there were ten thousand people in the stands, as if he were playing at Wembley, as if this would be the last concert in human history. Frequently, he would talk about the genesis of this or that song, citing verse and chapter about who wrote it, when, and why. He mentioned that when he first played Glasgow as a precocious teen, he was "stuck out there in a bed-and-breakfast at Sauchiehall Street." It just so happened that I was staying at a bed-and-breakfast on Sauchiehall Street, and not a particularly fancy one. Fame was in the twilight of his career; mine was right around four in the afternoon; but he still had the better digs. Never mind. Like Christopher Hogwood, like the Viola da Gamba Society, like the Rapiers, and yes, even like Talon, he was the keeper of the flame. The only difference was, Talon was keeping alive a flame that was still flickering elsewhere, one that would be no great loss if it finally went out.

After the concert, I chatted with members of the various bands outside the stage door. The lead guitarist of the Animals, who would die just a few months later, mentioned that the troupe's next concert was in Doncaster, in the north of England, and asked if I knew the best way to get there. It was an unusual question, since the Animals hailed from Newcastle, also in the north. I replied that I was from out of town, but in my experience, if you were playing in Scotland today and your next concert was in northern England tomorrow, you should probably start thinking about heading south.

I then asked one of the horn players in the Rebel Rousers what he thought of tribute bands like Talon, and his expression turned icy.

"I'd like to get my hands on them," he said. In his view, tribute bands were jackals that were taking bread off his table. There was honor in being a has-been; being a member of a tribute band was parasitical. I understood the sentiment, but could not entirely agree with it. As Talon was finishing up their concert in Stroud that memorable Friday evening, a woman as plump as Queen Victoria and an elderly man as old as Queen Victoria—with a cane, no less!—began shimmying and mouthing the words to "Life in the Fast Lane." If you were looking for folks living their lives in the fast lane, it would be hard to find a more unlikely place than Stroud. One part of me found this scene fraught with fabulous irony; one part of me found it disarmingly sweet. Music is supposed to be a healing medicament, and these hicks from the sticks certainly looked healed. It just went to show that when you ventured out into the wide, wide world looking for adventure, you never knew where you'd find it. When I was growing up in North Philadelphia, I had dreamed that I would wander in off the streets of a strange city on a frigid March morning and find myself in a museum of rare musical instruments where I would be personally serenaded on George Frideric Handel's harpsichord to the strains of Johann Sebastian Bach's sublime keyboard music. But I had never dreamed that I would wander in off the streets on a frigid March night and be entertained by an Eagles tribute band from North Wiltshire, Herefordshire, and Coventry.

Once again I was reminded that in Great Britain, you had to be prepared for anything. When I first read Lewis Carroll's *Alice in Wonderland* in my teens, I interpreted it as a chimerical fantasy about an innocent young girl who disappears down a rabbit hole and enters a phantasmagoric society populated by lunatics. Not until I married an Englishwoman and started visiting Old Blighty did I realize that Carroll was merely describing Britain the way she is. Once the heavy-duty weirdness starts, it never lets up. You can check out any time you like.

But you can never leave.

7

The Prince of Wails

Shortly before midnight on September 21, 1327, King Edward II was impaled on a red-hot poker, a barbarous indignity he did not survive. Exactly who came up with the idea of dispatching the inordinately unpopular and generally dissolute ruler in this monstrous fashion is the subject of considerable dispute, though it is undeniable that his wife, Isabella, sister of the King of France, and her lover, Roger Mortimer, approved of his execution, though not necessarily the manner in which it was carried out. (Their apologists later dismissed it as a prank that got out of hand.) Popular legend contends that the treasonous conspirators wanted to dispose of the king in a fashion that would make his death appear "natural," with no obvious external damage to his physical person. But the mortician's art would not reach a truly professional level for many centuries hence, and it quickly became obvious from the expression on the corpse's face that he had not died of lupus.

The murderers' heinous crime, carried out in a dark room at Berkeley Castle, backfired utterly. Despised during his lifetime for his effeminacy, his cavorting with the flamboyant Piers Gaveston, his abuse of the laws, and his decisive defeat by Robert the Bruce at Bannockburn, Edward II, the very first Prince of Wales, immediately became a martyr upon his death. Gloucester Cathedral, one of the most majestic edifices in all of Britain, was built largely with funds supplied by pilgrims from all over England who came to pay homage to the slain king. Just a few years later, Mortimer was executed upon orders of Edward III, a great king who recoiled at the way his father had been treated. Isabella herself was seized and imprisoned, then mercifully granted a stipend and permitted to drag out the rest of her life in obscurity, far from her native France.

Cinema buffs will recall that in *Braveheart,* Isabella was depicted as a sweet, vulnerable damsel with a poncey husband, and that she carried a torch for the ferociously virile William Wallace. But this is not true, as Wallace and Isabella (a mere thirteen when Wallace died) never met. It was just another one of these things that Mel Gibson, much, much shorter than the real Braveheart, made up. If the unlikely pair had become romantically involved, Isabella, known in her time as "the She-Wolf of France," would have been the first woman in history to have had sexual congress with one man who was hanged, drawn, and quartered; with a second who got a red-hot poker jammed into his bowels; and with a third who was hanged, drawn, quartered, castrated, beheaded, and had to watch his own intestines and heart being torn out while still breathing. She must have been a tigress in the sack.

The quaint, tragedy-soaked village of Berkeley is my favorite tourist attraction in all of Britain, and not just because I fancy blood and guts. No, I adore Berkeley because it fulfills all my needs as a world traveler. Every tourist worth his salt gradually develops a distinctive, personal style. The *obsessive* traveler wishes to gape in awe at every church built by Christopher Wren or every cathedral containing the remains of a duplicitous king. The *bibliophilic* traveler wants to visit the church where Carver Doone shot Lorna, the barren moors where Jane Eyre awaited her lonely death after abandoning Rochester, the courtroom where Jeffrey Archer was convicted of perjury, the Scottish castle where Madonna hired someone to help with the big words while writing her first children's book. The *economic* traveler wants to spend about forty-five minutes a day inspecting crypts, belfries, dungeons, and distinguished vestibules, and then spend the remains of the day getting juiced to the gills in pubs with suspiciously contrived names like The Frog & Ferkin or The Cock Up Your Beaver, or perhaps scarfing down cream teas at Mrs. Pinch-Penny's Toodle Hut. I am nothing if not an economic traveler.

All good English tourism and even the most casual Anglophilia are rooted in a love of bloodshed; almost every major tourist attraction is famous because someone died there in a spectacularly unpleasant fashion. But the wonderful thing about the sites of famous murders is that, unlike art museums, you can knock them off in a hurry. There's no reason to dawdle. The key to successful Anglo-travel, in my humble estimation, is to focus on one or two figures of surpassing historical interest, to learn everything you can about them, to quickly, expeditiously, visit the places where they were treacherously murdered, and then to whip down to the pub in time for the competitively priced carvery.

Most American tourists opt for Richard III, because he shares a psychic kinship with Lee Harvey Oswald and John Wilkes Booth, just as most tourists share a philosophical kinship with Oliver Stone. But my personal favorite among murdered English kings is Edward II, because his life and death provide a valuable lesson to us all. To wit: An awful lot of things have to go terribly wrong in your life in order for you to end up impaled upon a red-hot poker. Especially if you started out as the Prince of Wales. The miserable saga of Edward II, son of the mighty Edward Longshanks, the Hammer of the Scots, illustrates that no matter how many advantages you start out with as a child, you can still wind up with the short end of the stick. Or, in Edward's case, on it. I personally was not absolutely convinced that I was ever going to die until Princess Diana perished in that horrendous Parisian car crash. If individuals as cosseted and pampered as Diana and Edward II could check out at such an early age, what hope was there for the rest of us? Obviously, it did not help that they were both dumb.

But I digress, so let us return to Berkeley Castle. One of the main attractions of this rather demure medieval fortress is watching how the docents try to dance around the subject of Edward II's pitiful demise. One middle-aged lady referred to the tiny chamber in which the king was imprisoned as "the television room," where his captors could stare through a grate and watch *King for a Day*. This was part and parcel of the English tradition of tittering over the nation's grisly past.

As a rule, the docents merely report that the king had been murdered, without going into all the gory details. Then they divert visitors' attention away to the glorious carpets or imperial tapestries, or the hole the Roundheads shot through the outer battlements during the Civil War. They stifle the red-hot poker talk with sweeping generalizations about the famous paintings that adorn the walls of the castle in suspicious profusion. Or they invite visitors to marvel over Francis Drake's remarkable furniture, or Queen Bess's silk tapestry.

By my troth, I enjoy Elizabethan tapestries as much as the next fellow! But only for about twelve seconds. Then I want to get back to Edward II. What kind of relationship did he have with Queen Isabella? What triggered his bestial assassination? Was it something he said? Did his murderers think they could get away with it? How did they get him to keep still while he was being murdered? Is it true that the king's death sentence was written in a deliberately mispunctuated Latin note designed to protect Mortimer and Isabella from charges of regicide and general crimes against humanity? Was the murder the first example of an explicitly homophobic hate crime?

The guides are generally not interested in these queries. They seem to have forgotten the very thing that made Berkeley Castle famous. I notice a similar case of cultural amnesia at Gloucester Cathedral, about twelve miles away. There sits Edward's tomb right next to that of Osric, Primate of Mercia, who founded the first monastery on this site in 678. In short, when Edward was buried here, the edifice, or some part of it, was already more than six hundred years old. By comparison, Edward was a parvenu, a piker. (An aside: If you want to delve into all the gory details about the murder of

Edward II, don't look in the Diocese of Gloucester Book and Gift Shop. The last two times I stopped by, there was not a single volume about Edward II, much less the She-Wolf of France, in stock. This is like visiting the bookstore at the Little Big Horn and not being able to find any material about Crazy Horse, like browsing through the Books 'n' Things on Golgotha, without locating any written material about the Crucifixion, because the staff prefers to dwell on the more upbeat vignettes in Christ's storied career.)

But I am not the kind of man who lets tour guides off so easily. So back at Berkeley Castle, I invariably disrupt the canned spiels by asking to see the spike on which the unfortunate king was impaled. It seems like the sort of iconographic curiosity that could fetch a small fortune on eBay, ranking right up there with the arrow that felled Achilles or the spear with which the Roman centurion Longinus poked the Savior. The docents don't care for this sort of thing. They never do. They assume that tourists have come to see the Cumbrian soup tureens. At Cawdor Castle in Scotland, the docents go out of their way to stress that Macbeth never lived in the castle, that if we are in the market for seedlings transported from Birnam Wood we will have to look elsewhere.

Only once during my myriad visits do I find a tour guide who is willing to cite verse and chapter about the king's murder. Stiff and serious, but exhibiting the kind of subversive humor that is rarely found in the docent class, she informs me that no one wanted to take in the king's brutalized corpse after his assassination, as it seemed an unwise policy to get on the wrong side of Isabella and Mortimer, who were obviously capable of anything. She also explains that the assassins, one of whom was named Ogle, had pinioned the king with a small wooden table, though Christopher Marlowe in his play *Edward II* suggests that Edward may have been tricked into thinking he was getting some sort of harmless massage. (Marlowe himself was stabbed in the eye at age twenty-nine by one Ingram Frizer; historians have never been able to decide whether this homicide was the result of political intrigue, or stemmed from a disagreement over who should pay for the last flagon of mead.) The key question for me, of course, was how the news got out that Edward II had been impaled on a red-hot poker. Were his murderers going out of their way to publicize their cruelty as a warning to feisty rebels such as Rhys ap Grufydd? Or had they simply slipped up?

"Apparently there was quite a bit of discussion down at the local pub that evening," the tour guide replies, indicating that loose-lipped staff simply could not keep a lid on things back in that day and age. "'You'll never believe what they were up to at the castle tonight'—that sort of thing."

So, at long last, I had my answer.

MY WIFE DEPLORES THE DEAD-AND-BREAKFAST STYLE OF tourism I have cultivated over the years. But what she really dislikes is that my kids have acquired the same tastes. When you first marry a Brit, you are fascinated by the differences that give your conjugal pudding its special theme. But once the kids arrive, the gloves come off. Raising children becomes a pitched battle that lasts twenty years. The two of you are always dueling for emotional and cultural dominion of the household. I have always felt that one of the most difficult things for an English person raising children in America to accept is the fact that the children are going to grow up to be Americans. Generally speaking, the Brits do not assimilate. Unlike Eastern Europeans and refugees from even less appealing societies, the Brits do not turn up on American shores and suddenly start sporting Dallas Cowboys caps. Wherever they go, they set up the Raj. Your American house, heretofore furnished in the cool Danish Modern style, is suddenly cluttered with intimidating mahogany smoking cabinets that someone's Uncle Clive won in a card game with luckless Gurkhas in Lahore shortly before the very nasty Sepoy Rebellion of '57. Your son is named after a short British general who got his head chopped off by a nineteenth-century Islamic fundamentalist. Mysterious LPs with names like *Long John Baldry: Live in Norwich* or *The Very Best of the Bonzo Dog Band* gradually begin to push aside *Surrealistic Pillow* and *Axis: Bold As Love*. Spike Milligan DVDs, whose jokes you do not understand, turn up where the *Honeymooners* episodes used to be stored. And your collection of vintage Damon Runyon fables eventually cedes space on the bookcase to mildewed, two-hundred-year-old copies of the *Decline and Fall of the Roman Empire* that disintegrate in your very hands before you can get to the really good parts about Christians vs. Tigers or Nero poisoning his own mother.

The beleaguered American can only fight back with the insuperable weapon of reproduction. This is a flood the Redcoats cannot stanch. The expatriate Englishwoman bearing an American man's child finds herself in the same position as Geena Davis in *The Fly;* she had been impregnated by a monster and dreads the fiendish hybrid gestating in her womb. She hopes against hope that she will give birth to pasty-faced tykes who speak only when spoken to in lilting West Country accents, and who take enormous pleasure in small things. But then her progeny morph into Americans. They start acquiring things. They daydream about money. They lie about how many teeth they have lost so they can trick the tooth fairy into depositing a few extra quarters under their pillows. They clamor for a debit card at age four. They are loud and surly and always think they are right. They have no respect for tradition or authority. They scheme and conspire; they resort to cunning stratagems. They gamble on everything. They wish their kindergarten teachers dead, and they wish their deaths to be excruciating. They don't want to hear anything about saving for a rainy day or putting on their wellies; their idea of British civilization is Judas Priest.

As soon as my children were old enough to understand the nuances of British history, I took them to Berkeley Castle. Imbued with an inherent passion for the macabre that all intelligent Yank toddlers exhibit, they would gambol around the courtyard singing hastily improvised nursery rhymes:

Oh, Edward the Second was really dumb;
He got a spike right up the bum.

Or:

Edward the Second drew the joker
When Queen Isabella said, "Let's play poker."

Sad, but true.

■ ■ ■

THE ENCHANTING VILLAGE OF BERKELEY WOULD BE JUSTI-
fiably famous were it merely the site of a legendary king's horrid murder. But it has much more to offer. A hop, skip, and
jump from the castle stands the Edward Jenner Museum, the
house in which the celebrated late-eighteenth-century scien-
tist discovered how to render human beings immune to smallpox. He did this by infecting an eight-year-old boy with cowpox, a far less virulent disease, extracted from a stricken
milkmaid. Milkmaids, according to local legend, never fell
prey to smallpox once they had succumbed to cowpox. No
one knew why, least of all the milkmaids.

The guinea pig's name was James Phipps; he was the gardener's son. After he recovered from cowpox, Jenner tried to
infect him with smallpox, but the malignancy could gain no
purchase. And so the cure to one of mankind's greatest afflic-
tions was finally discovered. At the time, 10 percent of the
English population eventually fell prey to the ravages of this
monstrous disease, but thanks to Jenner's efforts, the dragon
was slain. One of my vague, long-range plans after I retire is
to find out what the gardener thought about all this; I am
equally interested in young James's views on the matter. Vari-
ola enthusiasts will certainly not be disappointed by their visit
to his house; it is truly a treat, filled with all sorts of fascinating displays. And, take note, clock watchers, Filofax lackeys,
and compulsive list makers: Have I mentioned that chez Jenner is but a two-minute stroll from Berkeley Castle?

Scientists are rarely famous for one discovery. Sensing that
their most revolutionary theories may one day be proven

wrong, the great scientists hedge their bets by achieving at least one other famous breakthrough. And so it was with Jenner, who, by dint of careful observation, established that newly hatched cuckoos surreptitiously polished off the eggs laid by their foster parents, a crime previously attributed to their own Machiavellian parents. Additionally, he proved that some species of birds migrate in the winter; previously, it had been widely believed that they hibernated during the cold months, perhaps underwater in local marshes and swamps. Jenner was also one of the first Englishman to fly a balloon in Britain, and apparently discovered the first plesiosaurus fossil on Stinchcombe Hill. Obviously, most of these achievements pale by comparison with his work on smallpox, but undeniably he was a great man, and his house is disarmingly pleasant, considering what it is famous for. I mention Jenner's sideline activities here simply because I am trying to close the sale.

Were this comely hamlet nestled on the banks of the Severn merely the site of a medieval king's brutal murder, and the building where the cure for one of the world's most deadly diseases was discovered, and the redolent copses where the unorthodox nesting habits of the cuckoo bird were uncrypted, it would be renowned the world over, at least by fatalities buffs like me. But Berkeley has yet another trick up its sleeve. Scant yards from the surprisingly cheerful castle and the even more engaging smallpox museum stands a Norman church built on the ruins of a Saxon church. The Minster Church of St. Mary the Virgin exudes the prerequisite beauty of all edifices of this genre. There is much to divert even the most demanding tourist: a Norman door dating from 1100, an inscribed Roman tile, and the lovely alabaster tomb of Lord Thomas of Berkeley, who was never punished for the heinous crime committed in his ancestral home, as he steadfastly maintained that he was out of town that particular evening. There is also reason to believe that both the ninth-century Abbess Ciolburga, widow of Ealdorman Ethelmund, and the Abbess Cynethritha, daughter of the redoubtable King Kenulf, may have dwelled on this very spot, though this could be hearsay.

Still not convinced that Berkeley is worth a side trip from such posh, overvisited localities as Oxford and Bath? Fine, let's roll out the pièce de résistance. For my money, the real jewel in this bucolic crown is the church graveyard containing the remains of Dicky Pearce. Pearce, who died in Berkeley Castle at the age of fifty-three on XVIII June, MDCCXXVIII, was the last court jester in English history. Unless you count Prince Charles. Entrusted with the admittedly difficult task of keeping the nobility amused, Pearce did not die a natural death. According to the inscription carved on his tombstone, Pearce "died in revelry." Beneath this statement read the words:

> *Here lies the Earl of Suffolk's Fool;*
> *Men called him Dicky Pearce;*
> *His folly served to make folks laugh,*
> *When wit and mirth were scarce.*

Adding to the marvels of this site is an epitaph penned by no less a luminary than Jonathan Swift, who eulogized his friend's passing with the words:

Poor Dick, alas, is dead and gone;
What signifies to cry?
Dickys enough are still behind,
To laugh at by and by.

I have read most of Dean Swift's work, and suspect that the greatest satirist of them all may have been having an off day when he took pen to paper in memory of his dearly departed friend. Still, it is a measure of the respect in which Pearce was held that a literary giant such as Swift would have written his epitaph. These days, if Billy Connolly or John Cleese or Eric Idle passed on, their epitaphs would probably be written by Eddie Izzard or Steve Martin, not a top gun like Margaret Drabble or Salman Rushdie. Yes, times change— and not always for the better!

As was the case with Edward II and Berkeley Castle, it was hard to pin down the locals on what the phrase "died in revelry" actually meant. The consensus among the sextons and docents I had badgered over the years was that the paid buffoon had keeled over drunk during one of his trademark pratfalls, and split his head on the sidewalk. This did not explain why no one else had stepped in to replace him. Was court jesting a badly paid profession? Had Pearce deliberately failed to groom his replacement, perhaps fearing that he might be prematurely ousted from the job by a feckless protégé? Was jestery already on its way out when Pearce breathed his last, succumbing to incursions from continental harlequins, *funambulistes, pucinellas,* castrati, or glib yes-men?

As I say, it was not easy to get answers to these questions.

Though the English are great devotees of historical curiosities, they tend to focus their attention on tried-and-true enigmas like Jack the Ripper's true identity and whether or not Avalon might have been located in what is now a truck lay-by in semirural Woodchester. English oddities enthusiasts tend to be far more interested in the alleged cat veneration practices of the Knights Templar or the sexual acrobatics of Morgan LeFay; by comparison, the tragic death of Dicky Pearce seems small beer indeed. I, on the other hand, have never had the slightest interest in mythological Britain, preferring to concentrate on the exploits of real people who lived real lives and died real deaths. Sometimes in revelry.

I suppose I could have dug up some ancient tome and painstakingly researched the rise and fall of the English court jester, but as a rule I prefer to rely on local legend and oral history. And so it was that I finally buttonholed that atypically informative tour guide at Berkeley Castle who told me precisely how the unfortunate Dicky Pearce met his fate.

"The lads got a bit drunk one evening and started tossing Dicky in a blanket," the middle-aged woman informed me. (The only people in all of Britain who actually know anything are the middle-aged women; younger women are not interested, older women have faulty memories; and the men are either liars or uninterested in anything but football.) "Somehow, things got out of hand and they accidentally tossed Dicky out of the minstrel's gallery. He landed on his head and died on the spot."

"And after that, they couldn't find anyone to replace him?" I inquired.

"That would be my assumption."

Far be it from me to suggest that the tweedy village of Berkeley can compare with Stonehenge for mystery, Tintagel for romance, York for grandeur, Lindisfarne for eeriness, the Lake District for natural splendor, or London for variety. I am merely saying that if you're squeezed for time or don't even like English history, you can't beat this bewitching hamlet. There are never any long lines at any of the historical sites; the graveyard is free; the castle has a well-stocked gift shop, and there are many fine tea shops and pubs nearby, as well as affordable lodgings for the dead-and-breakfast set. If you get to the castle as soon as it opens, then quickly gallop through the Jenner Museum, and make a short stop at Dicky Pearce's grave (you can skip the church; it's not *that* special), you can be in and out of the village in two hours flat. You'll have covered history, art, religion, regicide, tomfoolery, plague, ornithology, revolution, Norman ecclesiastical architecture, home decor, gardens, state-sanctioned sodomy, and Saxon mortuary in a single visit and can devote the rest of your trip to gambling, the theater, alcohol, or napping. Berkeley is the harried tourist's best friend: the weary pilgrim's one-stop cultural shopping center. It is also the site of the world's first commerical nuclear power plant. So put it on your list now.

8

10 Things I Hate About Britain.
No, Make That 20

The trusty old train was plowing north from Penzance, the old pirate's cove, to York, epicenter of the Plantagenet industry, when I noticed that we were chugging past Stroud. I had been in England for almost a month, and had finally fulfilled a lifelong dream of visiting rugged Cornwall, where the pasties are the size of bowling bowls, the roads have names like Market Jew Street, peripatetic barbers are available by mobile for "in-home haircuts," and the local radio station carries public service announcements like: "Contrary to reports, the Penzance Women's Choir has not disbanded, and is particularly looking for contraltos and mezzo-sopranos."

In nearby Truro, an old church had been transmogrified into a Pizza Express. The effect was jarring, but on the whole it was probably preferable to demolishing it and erecting an entirely new building. For a race that had spilled so much blood over religion down through the centuries, the English do not seem particularly devout, making it unlikely that the church would revert to its original function anytime soon. Moreover, modern commercial establishments tend to look awful. The problem with designing a new building anywhere in Britain is the competition. The Druids were here, and they worked very well with stone. So did the Romans. From the purely aesthetic point of view, Stonehenge, Bath, and the Merry Maidens of Land's End perhaps lack the rugged grandeur of the Tate Modern or the brutal splendor of the Lloyd's of London building. But they will probably last longer.

Truro's principal architectural showpiece was a nineteenth-century cathedral that was built too late to boast any valuable relics. Instead, it displayed a fake fur *amice,* handcrafted in the twentieth century, which was intended to be worn over a surplus or black cassock. The *amice* consisted of a short cape and cowl and was allegedly some sort of badge of honor sported by the *prehends* of Saint Endellion, as opposed to the *prehends* of Saint Wulfstan. Be that as it may, it looked like a dirty, hooded cap worn by a local motorcycle gang that, though handy with their fists, were a bit on the fey side.

The most striking objects in Truro Cathedral were the terra-cotta stations of the cross crafted by George Tinworth, a Victorian artist. Jesus and the rest of the Jews had been carved in a satisfactorily biblical style, but all the Roman centurions sported enormous mustaches that made them look like the Earp brothers: Wyatt Antony, Morgan Pilate, Virgil Aurelius, and Doc Caesar. Returning to Penzance from Truro, I passed beneath a number of underpasses embroidered with graffiti reading KERNOW VYS VYKEN: CORNWALL FOREVER; GET

OUT, SAXON SCUM!; WE ARE NOT ENGLISH!; CORNISH = WHITE NIGGERS, and my personal favorite, ALL ENGLISH SUCK DICK, which is neither polite nor statistically valid. In St. Ives I had even briefly been exposed to what I thought was a clear-cut case of Cornish pay phone abuse, when a nattering twit in an adjacent phone box yammered so long and loud into the mouthpiece that I hollered out: "Could you talk a little louder? They still can't hear you in Tintagel."

He apologized and explained that he was Dutch.

Cornwall covered, I was heading north to Durham, Lindisfarne, Edinburgh, and Glasgow, storied locales I had never visited because I always had stroppy children in tow and was forever stopping by to see some relative who lived in a West Country bungalow called "Alacrity" and might soon be moving to the south of France where it would be easier to land a role in an amateur production of *Can-Can*. But as the train scooted past the familiar hills of the Cotswolds, I felt a tinge of homesickness. I knew the Cotswolds like the back of my hand, and had spent many a joyful evening playing snooker with Tony, or feasting on Margaret's Brobdingnagian Yorkshire puddings, or listening to my old friend John Willoughby's tales of his epic leaps as a young morris dancer before the cruel ravages of Father Time forced him into the Stroud & District LVA Cribbage League.

Now, for the first time ever, I was traversing Stroud without stopping there. It was not a pleasant feeling; I felt like jumping off the train, just as I always did when I traveled from New York to Washington without stopping in my native Philadelphia. I had seen my niece and nephew grow up in Stroud. My daughter had lost her two front teeth—on Christmas, her birthday—in Cashes Green. I had repeatedly thrashed my brother-in-law at cribbage in Randwick. I had also beaten him at snooker. As a matter of fact, I had recently pummeled him 57–2 in a game of pub cricket, where the driver and the passenger count the legs on pub signs as "runs" and the bridges and overpasses as "outs." This was an astonishing feat, given that Tony knows all the local roads. But I was always the first one to spot The Coach and Horses or The Toff & Centipede. In short, Stroud had long since ceased to be an out-of-the-way tourist destination. It was, in some sense, home.

England, too, was, in some sense, home. From the English I had learned to take pleasure in small things, like a nice cup of tea or twenty minutes of direct sunlight. You never went into an English home, mine included, without being offered something to eat; the English were masters of the domestic niceties, an art that had eluded Americans, who can't stop talking about real estate and the college plans of their daft progeny long enough to fetch a dying man a glass of water. I loved the civility and humor of the English people; I loved their arch phrasing, infectious understatement, and delightful euphemisms. I loved companies with names like the Considerate Builder's Society, and adored newspaper accounts of soccer games beneath headlines such as "English Subs Sink Krauts." I loved their messy gardens, circuitous roads, stone cottages, ebulliently shabby pubs.

But I didn't love everything about England. One of the hazards of getting to know another country is that you eventually see all of its defects, glimpse the old gal without her makeup. This had happened to me before. Over the years, as my youthful love affair with France had succumbed to the slings and arrows of outrageous middle-aged misfortune, I had grown weary of its stupid politics, seditious unions, cretinous television, even more cretinous pop music, unwholesome obsession with food, and contempt for Americans— most particularly for those who did not speak French, making it impossible for them to feel the full force of their disdain. I still love France, but my love is no longer unconditional. I feel the same way about Britain.

My list of grievances starts with the twit. He went to either Oxford or Cambridge, a fact he never stops mentioning, but insists that he hated every second of it. If he'd had his druthers he would have been taking night school classes at a community college in Tasmania while driving a lorry or running guns to Nelson Mandela. But Maman insisted that he take a first in economics. He always waits to hear your opinion before expressing his, and looks like he is wearing a monocle even when he is not. His name is usually Jonathan or Adrian but should be Uriah or Polonius. He is either a journalist, a supernumerary in an art gallery, or a factotum for a politician who secretly hates the poor and is surprised to find out that the poor already know this. He is a master of rehearsed eccentricity; he feigns interest in the history of the soft pretzel, inquires whether any shops in the region specialize in lute repair, and delays everyone's dinner because he purports to have been taking in the exhibition of Marie-Antoinette's long-lost demitasses at the Maison de Porcelaine. He asks any English person now living in America when they first realized they were losing their accent, and acts surprised when he gets smacked or asked to leave before dessert. He uses the word *brilliant* as if it meant something, and supplements it with *extraordinary*, which means even less. He knows far too much about the unseemly events that transpired on March 4, 1597, at Lacock Abbey. He borrows money, sleeps on your couch for three weeks, never buys so much as a loaf of bread, and then complains about the heat or the absence of Arnold Bax from your record collection. He supports causes that do not matter, and opposes politicians whom everyone else already hates. He has exotic dietary requirements and, while not technically a vegetarian, acts like one. He wears peculiar footwear and owns no blue jeans. When you mention your friends in Bow, he pretends not to understand the word you are pronouncing, then exclaims, "Oh, you mean *Bow*." He believes that in a previous life he was the Keeper of the Royal Seal, the Marquis of Tavistock, or Ganelon Piggott-Tyne, the twenty-third Earl of Painswick. Elevating superciliousness to an art form, he exudes a maddening self-deprecation that camouflages an ingrained sense of his own superiority and, to borrow from the patois of the Valley Girl, he just totally deserves to have his grotty little neck wrung.

America does not have twits; there is no direct cultural correlation here. While the debutante is the American equivalent of the Sloane Ranger, the Cornish pasty the distant cousin of the knish, and Margaret Thatcher the British counterpart to Ronald Reagan, there are many things in England that do not exist in America. There is no equivalent to the soccer hooligan in America, just as there is no British counterpart to the Crips and the Bloods. The United States has no one quite like Mick Jagger; Britain has no one quite like Johnny Cash. There is no British Woody Guthrie, though

Billy Bragg would like it otherwise; there is no American Charles Dickens, though Tom Wolfe would like to think there is. Marmite does not, and could not, flourish in America. American men do not fantasize about spanking meter maids. The English do not tip, and when they do, they tip badly; the Scots are worse. American restaurants never turn you away because the food has run out; Americans would never eat fish wrapped in newspaper. By and large, the British do not understand the social lubricant of naked, unalloyed greed. And so on. The twit seems to be a species that the British Isles not only invented, but reluctantly beatified; the closest we get is the fuddy-duddy, the nincompoop, the noodge, or what was once referred to as "the smacked ass." You say "potahto"; we say "potayto." You have the twit. We have the asshole.

Britain also has choreographed working-class rage, which does not play well in America, even among the enraged working classes. When I was a boy growing up in a housing project built by Grace Kelly's father, I did not resent the fact that Grace Kelly didn't live there with me; I wanted to grow up to live in a house like Grace Kelly's. Rabble-rousing politicians in the United States ultimately find that class warfare is a dead-end street because everyone in America wants to grow up to be rich, and if you spend your formative years despising the class you secretly want to infiltrate, you'll spend your dotage back in the housing project. I agree with John Lennon that "a working-class hero is something to be," but you don't want your kids to be working-class heroes. You want them to go to work for Morgan Stanley and corral a dandy pension.

I felt the full brunt of traditional English working-class

rage one night in South London when I was making a short film for Channel 4 entitled *My Fair Hugh*. The premise was simple: I was cast as a carapaced, deeply cynical American journalist whose only chance of reviving his moribund career was to visit London, learn to impersonate Hugh Grant, and hopefully set up an interview with Grant's inamorata Liz Hurley. The movie followed the standard *My Fair Lady* template, as I gradually mastered Grantian diction by repeating the phrase, "In Basingstoke, Bath, and Battersea, bad boys are born to be buggered." The film featured all manner of turgid Merchant-Ivorian lines like: "I have always thought of myself as a bit of an *Inglese-Italianato*" and "Lydia and Hermione: Please tell Simcox to move the pianoforte out onto the veranda; the boathouse is all at sixes and sevens."

The emotional climax of *My Fair Hugh* was originally written as a scene where the faux Hugh Grant, no longer wishing to be the real Joe Queenan, is beaten to a pulp by soccer hooligans outside Arsenal's pitch at Highbury. But because the producer Richard Jobson was a bit tight with a buck, the scene was shot on Asylum Road in the South London pub where the Millwall football club's supporters hang out. A taxi-cab driver Richard had met in his travels volunteered to provide the pub as a backdrop for the denouement, and also agreed to bring in a group of his mates. I did not know this when I arrived at the pub in my pink shirt, foppish hair, and silly eyeglasses. But before I ventured out that evening, I phoned a London friend and asked if it was a good idea to go into Millwall's pub and say things like: "The reason everyone hates you is not because of your appalling clothes and hideous accents or because you never shot grouse from your windows at Trinity, but because you lack refinement." My friend knew a bit about football; he did not think it was a good idea at all. I also asked him if the lads would take my comments in the spirit in which they were intended if I added: "Be you blithe and bonny, converting all your cares and woes into hey nonny-nonny." He mulled it over for a minute, noting in passing that the club's supporters had adopted the motto: "No one likes us; we don't care," and then said, "Millwall supporters don't have much of a sense of humor."

We arrived at the pub in a fleet of vehicles and immediately plummeted headlong into the abyss. A gang of postmodern street urchins descended on the caravan and civic-mindedly reported that there had been a shocking amount of vandalism in the area in recent times, and that it would behoove us to hire them to protect the cars from the depredations of roving villains. We forked over twenty pounds. Inside, the pub was filled with central-casting football fans. I felt a bit out of place in my prissy getup, given that Millwall was synonymous with hooliganism and its twin sister, violence. But I didn't feel nearly as uncomfortable as the Scottish stylist, the Jewish line producer, and the Pakistani gofer. Millwall supporters don't care much for the Scots. They can't stomach Jews. But they really hate people named Mohammed.

Jobson's arrangement was this: He would pay for all the drinks, and the Millwall fans would play themselves. We shot the scene quickly, as there was no telling how soon the belligerent young men in the pub would weary of our ironic temperament and cannibalize us. What I remember most about the evening was a feeling of utter fatigue with their lockstep proletarian rage, which they wore like a uniform, and a general lack of respect for their finely manicured aura of latent menace. They were bullies, and, like all bullies, they were cowards. They had strength in numbers, but so did the Mongols. It didn't take any courage for two dozen lions of Millwall to intimidate short Jewish men or even shorter Scottish lassies; it took courage to venture into their pub if your name was Mohammed. English soccer hooligans need to spend a week in the South Bronx or twenty minutes in East L.A., if they could last that long.

ON THE SUBJECT OF ANGRY YOUNG MEN, THIS SEEMS LIKE A good place to say a few words about the Pre-Raphaelites. The Pre-Raphaelite Brotherhood was founded by six young painters and one young writer in September 1848. The most important members were William Holman Hunt, Dante Gabriel Rossetti, and John Everett Millais, in whose Bloomsbury home the movement was spawned. Inventors of the dreaded "mission statement," the group set itself the specific task of eradicating the artifice and general mannerism they believed had gradually crept into Western art since the fifteenth century. Unlike later generations of painters, who instinctively revile *anyone* who painted better work than they have and had the nerve to do it centuries earlier, the Brotherhood had a specific ax to grind with Raphael. In launching their counterinsurgency, they singled out his *Transfiguration* (which hangs in the Vatican) as "a painting which should be condemned for its grandiose disregard of the simplicity of truth, the pompous posturizing of the Apostles, and the unspiritual attitudinizing of the Savior." Then they went out and painted canvases that would one day be snapped up by Andrew Lloyd Webber.

Ostensibly devoted to uncompromising realism and the transmission of badly needed moral exempla to the middle classes, the Pre-Raphaelites (and enthusiastic co-conspirators like Edward Burne-Jones) ended up painting raftloads of waterlogged Ophelias, emaciated maidens, arsenic-swilling poets, and overdressed Messiahs. They reveled in befuddled sheep, disoriented virgins, and anything to do with Merlin; they gave their works titles like *The Baleful Head, Phyllis and Demophoon,* and *The Awakening Conscience.* They never saw a shade of purple they didn't like; the figures in their paintings wore woeful, histrionic expressions that would later be popularized by the now-forgotten silent-film star Theda Bara. I know of no Pre-Raphaelite paintings that are not vulgar and stupid; they make Boucher and Fragonard look like gritty urban realists. They are easily the worst painters that ever lived.

The Pre-Raphaelites did not limit their crimes to the world of pigmentation. They wrote books. They gave lectures. They set up schools. They published a journal called *The Germ.* They were philosophers and poets, prophets and proselytizers, seers and shamans, neologists and nitwits. They were deadly serious and never said anything funny, especially after Rossetti's girlfriend, who'd been rehearsing for death since childhood, expired. Their influence can be found in everything from the cover of Molly Hatchet's 1981 LP *Take No Prisoners* to the reenactment movement, where grown women with homes, children, driver's licenses, and possibly even jobs spend entire weekends pretending to be the Lady of the Lake

or Parsifal's kid sister Rowena. Wherever there is a nineteen-
year-old boy who dismisses Rembrandt as a pimp, wherever
there is a twenty-two-year-old girl who believes that society
worked better in the days of Andromeda and Lilith, wherever
there is a painter who thinks that he and only he has everything figured out, you can detect the lurking specter of the
Pre-Raphaelites. There is much to be said for young people
warring with their parents and even with their grandparents,
but these self-absorbed poltroons had the nerve to demean the
Renaissance, the single greatest event in recent human history. Here, they were out of their weight class; the Pre-
Raphaelites' picking a fight with the celestial Raphael is like
the church tabby cat getting into the ring with a Bengal tiger.

Art has always proven a problematic issue in England,
where the genre is basically feared and disliked. Artists are
expected to put on a show; painting is secondary. The English
love it when an artist makes a fool of himself by dressing up
as a schoolgirl or suspending a sheep in embalming fluid; it
confirms their theory that artists need to be institutionalized.
When the English buy art, they expect it to be horrendous,
and will accept no substitute. In St. Ives, the gallery owners
could pass for gangsters and the painters look like they're on
their way to a Halloween party where everyone has to dress
up as Vincent van Gogh. With so many weekend Watteaus
prowling around St. Ives, Newlyn, and Penzance, garbed as if
they have just purchased their berets and scarves from the
Pepé Le Pew Catalog, you can't tell whether they are painters
or Che Guevara impersonators: Everybody's wearing fishermen's caps except the fishermen.

Ghastly paintings have long been a staple of provincial

museums throughout Britain. Consider the Royal Museum and Art Gallery in Canterbury, where the curators seem to have assigned themselves the task of hanging every wretched nineteenth-century painting they could lay their hands on, perhaps as an ironic counterpoint to the magnificent thirteenth-century architecture right down the street. These cultural morgues are always festooned with hideous late Impressionist works like *It Was the Time of Roses* by Sir David Murray, RA, PRI, RSW, 1849–1933. Nobody with that many titles after his name ever produced a good painting. Also on hand are works such as *Romeo and Juliet at Reculver, Kent,* by Walter Richard Sickert, RA. When I first saw this dreadful canvas in March 1976, I had an inkling that the painter might be a mass murderer; years later this suspicion was confirmed when Patricia Cornwall wrote her potboiler *Portrait of a Killer,* proving that Sickert was in fact Jack the Ripper. You only needed to look at his brushstrokes to see it.

British museums are very good on gigantic cows, horses with buttocks that would give a rhino a run for his money, and bewitching house pets. They positively adore artworks with names like *The Broken Tryst, Eve Tempted, Bright Eyes,* and *Toilers of the Sea,* but have a particular soft spot for works like *A Persian Prince, His Slave Bringing Him Sherbert,* and *General Sir David Baird Discovering the Body of the Sultan Tippoo Sahib, After Having Captured Seringapatam on the 4th of May, 1799.* There is no painting too bad to be hung, and no concern about what it is displayed next to. Directly opposite a glorious painting by Turner, in the National Gallery of Scotland in Edinburgh, you can find a Hallmark Card rendering of a wee doggie entitled *The Portrait of His Favorite Dandie*

Didmont Terrier. Apparently, by terms of the donor's will, the painting must hang in this spot in incongruous perpetuity, serving as an intellectual way station for roving Philistines who find the Constables, Giorgiones, Bellinis, and Gainsboroughs just too, too cerebral.

MANY OF BRITAIN'S PROBLEMS TODAY ARE THE SAME ISSUES IT was grappling with hundreds of years ago. In anno Domini 2004, the British people are fiercely divided about the future of the royal family, but this was true eight hundred years ago when King John was forced to meet the grumbling nobles at Runnymede. Those who would like to see the royal family pensioned off, or at least furloughed, are always complaining that Prince Charles is a nattering twit, but this was true of Edward II, Henry VI, and George IV.

It is not going too far to say that no matter how hard they try, some societies can never solve a particular problem. There are no great French-Canadian painters. There are no world-class Bolivian gymnasts. Inuits have yet to produce an interest rate forecaster to be reckoned with. As for Americans, they are generally not good at anything that involves class, tradition, or taste, and cannot relax unless they are drinking, taking drugs, or embezzling their dying mother's life savings so they can short Microsoft.

This brings us to one of the British people's salient failings. It is a serious problem; it is a problem that should have been sorted out centuries ago; yet it is a problem that shows no signs of being seriously addressed. Here, with the reader's indulgence, I would like, once again, to bring the redoubtable

Saxons into the discussion. At the dawn of the seventh century, civil discord reigned in Britannia. The Romans were long gone and unending civil war was the plight of a troubled people. Finally, a dark picture began to brighten when King Ethelbert of Kent married Bertha, daughter of the reigning Frankish king, who was himself a descendant of the mighty warrior Clovis, whom many historians credit with inventing the very idea of France.

Bertha was a Christian; Ethelbert still placed his faith in Thor, Odin, and, to a lesser extent, Loki. For proto-Machiavellian political reasons, Ethelbert now unexpectedly converted to Christianity. In theory, this would help to ease tensions between the English in the east and the British in the west. Seeking to reach an official accommodation with the warlike and in many ways implacable British, who claimed to descend from both the Celts and the Romans, Ethelbert and the newly arrived Saint Augustine convened a summit conference in the Severn Valley near Wales. It was their earnest hope that the entire southern portion of the island could now be united once and for all under the banner of militant Christianity.

The parley failed, for several reasons. According to Winston Churchill's *A History of the English-Speaking Peoples,* one intractable problem was the feuding parties' disagreement over the official date of Easter. A second was the arrogance and intransigence of the British bishops. But the main stumbling block was a furious and ultimately irresoluble debate over hairstyles. Augustine, a transparent tool of the papacy, favored the traditional Roman tonsure, which involved shaving the top of the head to effect what the Normans would later derisively refer to as *la coupe Friar Tuck.* The British bishops, still laboring under the stylistic hegemony of the Druids, preferred shaving from the center of the head all the way out to the ears, leaving but a tiny fringe on the forehead. According to Churchill, it was "a choice of the grotesque." The conference disintegrated with the two sides now hating each other more at the end than they had at the beginning. The island promptly reverted to hundreds of years of savage, internecine war.

Contrary to what the public might think, this seminal tragedy demonstrates that the British problem with hair did not begin with Rod Stewart. It has been there from the beginning. Anyone spending any length of time in Britain is aware that hair is a problem the natives have never mastered, just as the French have never mastered plumbing, the Germans humility, the Japanese humor, or the Mormons monogamy. The British introduced the preposterous Prince Valiant look centuries ago and have kept it alive through the ministrations of the young Mick Taylor, the middle-aged Dave Davies, and the paleolithic Bill Wyman; it was the otherwise dignified David Bowie who introduced the dreaded mullet. Porcine, middle-aged women with schoolgirl bangs make Britain an optical nightmare from Land's End to the Shetlands, and the spiky bird's-nest look fancied by both Rod Stewart and Ron Wood is still regularly spotted on public transit users everywhere. Early practitioners of the comb-over, which was brought to vertiginous heights on American shores by Rudy Giuliani, the English are also responsible for perfecting both the rural Mohawk and the *Look, Mom: The Apaches Got Me!* shaved head.

The Aryan National Ninny look is particularly worthy of

discussion. In the good old days, you could easily identify a man with a shaved head as a Nazi, a neo-Nazi, or a Manchester United supporter. Today, he could be anyone from a certified public accountant to an assistant art director at *Arena* magazine. The self-inflicted scalping is a prime example of modern cognitive dissonance: It is neither left nor right; neither gay nor straight; neither fish nor fowl. It confuses an issue that is already confused enough. The prematurely shaved head is a powerful symbol of tonsorial cowardice, in which the rapidly balding male seeks to launch a preemptive strike against Time's follic ravages by simply throwing in the towel. If women started doing this in any great numbers, the race would die out in a week. Either that or an army of Sinéad clones would have to really start shaking their moneymakers.

The Tate Britain, the repository of Britain's greatest home-grown artistic treasures, is a very fine museum indeed. But it also serves an important anthropological function, housing a powerful visual record of the most insidious hairstyles of the past. Particularly terrifying examples include Gerard Soest's *Henry Howard, 6th Duke of Norfolk*, in which the nobleman appears to have a filthy mink stole draped around his head. To this can be added Lemuel Francis Abbott's portrait of the engraver Francesco Bartolozzi, where the unfortunate man seems to be topped off with a desiccated dust mop. William Holman Hunt's *Claudio and Isabella* features a man with bright red hair parted right down the middle, evoking the grooming influence of Bozo the Clown. *William Murray, 1st Earl of Mansfield* appears to be sporting a toilet seat atop his head in the portrait by the American expatriate John Singleton Copley, and *Sir John Fielding* by Nathaniel Hone marks the first known appearance of the extraneous Rugby Union headband, used to restrain hair that does not need restraining.

Dante Gabriel Rossetti, whose influence on Mary Elizabeth Mastrantonio's Promethean Afro in *Scarface* cannot be overlooked, deserves mention here, as do Henry Lamb and the aforementioned Millais, from whom the band Jethro Tull was to draw so much inspiration. Other disturbing stylings include the ludicrous pigtails that are to be found in several works by Sir Joshua Reynolds and James Barry; two centuries later, these would exert a profound grooming influence on the beloved Aussie Wimbledon champion Pat Cash. Perhaps the most electrifying portrait of all is John Webber's rendering of Captain James Cook, in which the great explorer seems to have wings protruding from his skull; Cook was beaten to death and possibly eaten by superstitious aboriginals in Hawaii in 1779, and frankly I think it may have been the hair that pushed them over the edge. According to a Blue Bird guide I briefly chatted up in the Old Tate, the Stuarts apparently thought they looked positively smashing in their preposterous wigs; but, of course, she also insisted, despite all evidence to the contrary, that Turner could draw, and may have merely been shielding the royal family from revisionist abuse.

I am certainly not suggesting that all Brits take their cues from homegrown painters—the sinister scalpers outside West End theaters look more like Goya's cretins—but these artists certainly cast a wide hairnet. In his famous portrait of Samuel Johnson, Sir Joshua Reynolds seems to have deliberately stapled a small but obtrusive sheep to the great satirist's head, perhaps while the subject was busy making fun of Shakespeare. In his idiosyncratic *Dictionary*, Johnson declared that a "fishing rod" was "a stick and a string, with a hook at one end and a fool at the other." He might have expanded his definition of the word *fool* to describe anyone who would pay Sir Joshua Reynolds to paint his portrait. Reynolds, a self-promoting reactionary who treated Gainsborough abysmally, caught a chill in the Sistine Chapel and went deaf. Frankly, I would have preferred that he'd caught glaucoma and gone blind. So, I'm sure, would Samuel Johnson.

IN MY VIEW, ALL TRAVEL IMPRESSIONS ARE COMPLETELY SUB-jective. Even the most boring places can be fun if the stars are in the proper alignment. There are few places in Britain that are objectively bad; it depends on your point of view. I once spent a delightful day in Weston-super-Mare frolicking on the beach with children. My wife bought the game little tykes matching sets of bright red Wellington boots and they spent the entire afternoon wading in the mud, foolishly hoping to catch a fleeting glimpse of the ocean. They were not successful, but were cheered by the promise of a free evening pantomime at the Sandringham Hotel. The panto did not materialize; the sign was about seventy-five years out of date; but by this point they were asleep. This allowed me to duck downstairs to the hotel bar, where a local pianist delivered rousing versions of "I'll Be Seeing You in Apple Blossom Time" and, in my honor, "The Yellow Rose of Texas." Back in those days, I still drank, so I did not take offense. This glorious day in an inglorious locale was not an isolated incident. I have spent many pleasant evenings with friends in lugubrious Bow. Brighton I have found to be intermittently diverting.

Margate is not without its delicate allures. Gloucester is dull, but at least it has the cathedral. Bristol is duller, but at least it has a suspension bridge. Travel writers always act as if there are objective standards for judging the places they visit, but most of the time they rain fire and brimstone on a harmless municipality simply because they could not get laid or the magazine sponsoring the trip would not throw in enough expense money to cover the Scandinavian Natural Blond Pre-Op TV Headmistress: Call Me If You Dare! (Yes, twelve centuries later, savage Vikings are still invading, and they are still inflicting pain on the locals.) I have had wonderful times in some of the least idyllic places in Britain. Cardiff. Minehead. Glasgow. Brixton. When the sun is shining in Britain, anywhere can be paradise.

Well, almost anywhere. In my experience, the stars have never been in the proper alignment when I was in Birmingham. The accent is horrible. The inhabitants are morose. The beer is ghastly. The downtown is hideous. The suburbs are grim. The art museum boasts a huge collection of Pre-Raphaelite paintings and for this reason alone, a cordon sanitaire should be established around the entire metropolis. *The New York Times* recently ran an article declaring that Birmingham was quietly shedding its dowdy image and preparing to take its place in the sun, but I think the reporter got on the wrong train, ended up in Manchester, and confused the two cities. I was almost run over by a lorry in 1976 while visiting Birmingham; I found out that the Queen Mother had died while sitting in the bus station in Birmingham; I got violently ill at a screening of a film about postwar vampires while I was in Birmingham. Nothing good has ever happened to me in Birmingham; I suspect I am not the only person who feels this way. It was perhaps unforgivable that the Germans tried to destroy the city during the Blitz, but the least they could have done was finish the job.

Are there any other things about Great Britain that really get up my nose? Well, how much time do you have? I have already made my feelings pretty clear about Druids, Andrew Lloyd Webber, and the Pre-Raphaelites, which are basically the same thing, and am not all that taken with London accents, or any of that malarkey about the Raj. I despise English expats who trash their own country because the weather is so much nicer in Seattle; anyone who would rather live in Seattle than die in Salisbury deserves to be flogged. I deplore faux Dickensian pub owners and traditional morning radio deejays. These are the lovely lads who feign a fawning concern for the tastes of their invisible but presumably Jurassic Era listeners, acting as if they are custodians of some imperiled national dream. Then they play "Fernando."

Language itself is an obstacle to communication in the Sceptered Isle. When the Welsh long ago decided that they did not want to be like everybody else, they retreated into a rough, inaccessible terrain that could only be mastered with the greatest difficulty, and into a language that could not be mastered at all. When the English reached a similar decision about the modern world, they decided to take refuge in an idiosyncratic idiom that no one else could decipher without access to a modern-day Rosetta stone. Basically, they elected to perfect a manner of speaking that camouflaged their true feelings beneath a veneer of rehearsed civility. (This presupposes that the English have real feelings, a theory that is itself debatable.) When the English say that someone is terribly *clever,* what they really mean is that the person is to be congratulated for an unusual ability to get things done despite the absence of any discernible native intelligence. Cleverness in a fellow human being, almost always a foreigner, resembles the shocking ability of the bear to dance. That the bear does not dance well is a matter of no great concern; the fact that the bear dances at all is a source of shock and amazement. The term *clever* is frequently used to describe small children, industrious immigrants, and Americans.

Like the Welsh, the English use expressions that no one else can ever mouth with any real confidence that they are making themselves understood, much less that they fully understand what they are saying. The English language thus becomes a sort of elaborate code that only the most skillful linguist can crack. The term *cheers* does not actually mean anything; its full range stretches from "Thanks" to "Would you mind getting your foot off my luggage?" The dreary neologism *brilliant* denotes everything from "Great idea" to "I don't really want to speak to you anymore; this conversation is at an end." Terms like *sunshine* and *mate* are equally ambiguous; sometimes they are completely innocuous, sometimes they contain a subtext of menace. I have never used the terms *naff, prat,* and *ripe wally;* I do not know what they mean; I am not sure I want to find out. None of these expressions can ever be spoken with any confidence by English speakers from other climes; when Pakistani shopkeepers use pseudo-affectionate terms like *dear* when chatting with customers, they merely sound ridiculous.

The English are ceaselessly inventing new terms that

make an American's skin crawl. "Have you had any *joy* finding that phone number I asked you about?" is the kind of arch, precious turn of phrase that evokes a Sloane Ranger trendiness and vapidity that has no equivalent in the American tongue. It is the twenty-first-century version of "smashing" and "jolly good show"; it is simultaneously theatrical and inane. It is the kind of phrase that delineates the distinction between the classes; one is never surprised to hear someone named Pippa or Nicola or Sasha inquire if you have had any joy; it is almost never heard in the mouths of rugby players, supermarket cashiers, or people named Mohammed. On a personal note, I have never had any joy locating a phone number, tracking down a Web site, or making a reservation for dinner, and I do not expect things to change anytime soon. Mine is a joyless existence, and I am more than happy to keep it that way.

For a nation that gave the world both Shakespeare and Milton, the English are surprisingly incommunicative. They rarely mean what they say; they rarely say what they mean; by and large they would prefer to sit in a corner and be left alone with their shepherd's pie. It is not merely a case of using language to frustrate conversation; they often give the impression that they would rather not speak at all. Even in emergencies of one sort or another, they prefer to converse only when it is absolutely necessary, and will not engage strangers in conversation unless a gun is put to their heads.

An illustration: I had just lost a one-pound coin in a public phone booth half a mile from Paddington railroad station. As this was perhaps the fifth one-pound coin I had lost that week, London phone boxes being notoriously confiscatory, I yanked out a Bic pen and tried to pry the coin loose from the aperture in which I had deposited it. I had no joy; the pen snapped off at the nib. Harried, I jammed it into the outer pouch of my stylish shoulder bag and continued my trip to historic Paddington station, which figures prominently in one of Agatha Christie's most famous mysteries. Along the way, I crossed paths with at least two merchants, a ticket taker, an information desk clerk, and several dozen people on the tube.

Clambering aboard the crowded train, I asked an unpleasant-looking senior citizen if the seat adjoining hers was vacant. I did not really want to sit next to her; she looked like she had been jilted at the altar fifty years earlier and was still chasing rats away from the wedding cake. But my feet hurt and the seat was empty. She stared at my face and said that yes, technically speaking, the seat was available, but her bag was lodged in the space where my feet would go, so she advised me to look elsewhere. I queried at least six other passengers about seating arrangements until I finally commandeered a vacant space right across from a mousy-looking middle-aged woman. Then I hurried off to the restroom. Two men standing outside the toilet informed me that it was occupied, but this proved not to be the case. Forcing in the door, I glanced at the mirror and noticed that a bright blue patch of ink adorned my nose, giving me a distinctive clownlike appearance. There were also splotches of ink on my eyebrows, cheeks, earlobes, and neck, and my hands were a complete mess. I had spoken to no fewer than fifteen people in the previous half hour, and had made eye contact with two score more, yet not one person could shed their congenital shell of timidity and self-effacement to tell me that I had ink all over my nose. Trained from birth to mind their own goddamn business, my interlocutors and fellow travelers obviously felt that it was not their lookout to tell a complete stranger that he had bright blue ink smeared all over his nose; if a grown man wanted to tart himself up in this unorthodox manner, that was his prerogative. Perhaps, in their minds, it was a new fashion. Perhaps it was the result of a defective rhinoplasty. Perhaps it was some sort of nasally oriented religious iconography. Maybe it was a newfangled tattoo. But at the end of the day, not to put too fine a point on it, it had nothing to do with them.

Allowing another human being to suffer a misfortune not of his own making illustrates how civility can surreptitiously transmute itself into indifference. A Canadian would have told me that I had ink on my face. A Russian would have told me I had ink smeared all over my nose. Any Welshman worth his salt would have muttered something about the case of the exploding Bic pen. Even the most timid American would have suggested, "You might want to do something about that piehole, pilgrim."

But the English just sat there. All the way to the Cotswolds.

Bastards.

OF ALL MY RESERVATIONS ABOUT GREAT BRITAIN, HOWEVER, none outstrips my dread of what befalls our two societies when hands reach across the water. Perhaps the greatest drawback of sharing a common language, and, to a certain extent, a common culture is that it facilitates, and perhaps even encourages, collusion between the worst people in Britain and the worst people in America. While it is true that Adolf Hitler and Benito Mussolini managed to bridge the language barrier and forge a bond that briefly threatened to extinguish the flickering candle of civilization, such sinister international liaisons infrequently occur at the cultural level. Shackled by linguistic shortcomings, Roberto Benigni has never joined forces with Robin Williams to make a musical version of *Schindler's List,* nor has Johnny Hallyday, the French Elvis, ever locked arms with Yanni, the Greek Yanni, in a Franco-Hellenic version of *Butch Cassidy and the Sundance Kid.*

But in the English-speaking world, such satanic alliances are not only possible, but in some instances preordained. Drawn together by some terrifying force of cultural magnetism that they themselves cannot resist, it is inevitable that Elton John and Billy Joel mount a concert tour together, convinced that by pooling their malignant resources they can alchemically generate a hybrid genre of entertainment that is infinitely more repellent than anything they could produce separately. It is precisely this imperative that impels the epic burnout Eric Clapton to seek out the storied has-been B. B. King so they can concoct an Anglo-American blues summit that is a dozen times more flatulent than anything they could initiate all by their dark and dirty loneselves. Just as the philosophical soul mates Tony Blair and Bill Clinton are drawn together by an almost conjugal smarminess, it is impossible for Rod Stewart to resist the siren song of *The Great American Songbook*. Left to his own devices, Stewart could only do so much harm to our shared musical heritage. But armed with these hokey chestnuts from days of yore, the most famous Small Faces alumnus of them all becomes the Antichrist himself.

Those of us who lay awake at night dreading fresh cases of Anglo-American collaboration live in fear that we will emerge from our slumber and read in the morning papers that Depeche Mode has merged with Chicago to form a multi-generational has-been supergroup, or that Emma Thompson and Meryl Streep have signed up with Ismail Merchant and James Ivory to film a bittersweet paean to Edwardian hookers entitled *Tarts in Crinoline*. Perpetually fearful of recidivist musical horrors, we hold our breath hoping that rumors of a Paul McCartney–Michael Jackson reunion—*Ebony and Ivory at San Quentin*—are false. Psychologists refer to this obsessive terror as Minogue Minnelli syndrome, the all-encompassing fear that unless our respective governments intervene, the collusion between two—or three—of our nations' most odious female performers cannot be avoided.

The most recent example of this cultural war crime is the unholy alliance of Boy George and Rosie O'Donnell. Boy George is a sterling example of modern civilization's worst innovation: the precocious has-been, the flamboyant pop idol whose star goes into eclipse at an early point in his career, and who then spends the next sixty years of his life reminding his countrymen of the appalling mistakes of their youth. Rosie O'Donnell is an extremely powerful comedienne, actress, and talk-show host who was briefly known as the Queen of Nice before revealing her true colors as the Spawn of Baal. Had

Boy George been born in Lithuania and Rosie O'Donnell in Beijing, their paths would never have crossed and civilization would have been spared their pitiless depredations. But because they are both English speakers, and because they are both pathologically vile, it was inevitable that they should unite to bring the woeful musical *Taboo* to Broadway.

Broadway, whatever its faults, did not deserve this. Once the incubator of great talents, the Great White Way succumbed to the cultural occupation forces of Andrew Lloyd Webber in the 1970s and 1980s and has never been the same. Like the bloodthirsty Napoleon hacking his way across Europe, Lloyd Webber had crushed the theater district beneath his iron heel, serially inflicting such hecatombs as *Jesus Christ Superstar* (the Battle of Austerlitz), *The Phantom of the Opera* (Jena), *Starlight Express* (the Battle of the Pyramids), *Sunset Boulevard* (Wagram), and *Cats* (Borodino). Though Lloyd Webber eventually met his Waterloo with *Whistle Down the Wind*, which closed before ever reaching Broadway, the carnage he left in his wake could not be undone. Indeed, it is my earnest belief that Lloyd Webber, who has been ominously quiet for several years, is merely biding his time like the Little General at Elba, and that the Anglo-American musical community will never be truly safe until he is permanently exiled to a small rock in the South Atlantic. This is not merely a dream; it is a suggestion.

Little needs to be said about *Taboo* other than that it deals with the adventures of the young Boy George, and therefore cries to the heavens for divine retribution. Yet it is a measure of the mutual depravity evinced by Boy George and Fat Girl O'Donnell that even after it was apparent that the musical would lose a fortune, the pair refused to close it for months upon months until $10 million had disappeared forever. Like Hitler issuing absurd, unenforceable commands from the bunker long after the war had been lost, O'Donnell and George refused to cut their losses, preferring to inflict as much pain on as many innocent people as time and money would permit, regardless of the consequences. I pale in the presence of such remorseless cruelty. I pale. And while I recognize that much of the responsibility for this nightmare resides with the odious American producerette, the lion's share of the blame rests with the British. As has so often been the case in Anglo-American relationships, we merely provided the money; you provided the murder weapon.

And for this I can never forgive you.

9

Sweep Through the Heather

No one should attempt writing about Great Britain without first consulting Paul Theroux's majestic *The Kingdom by the Sea*. The book, published in 1983, recounts the author's long walk around Britain's coast during the Falklands War. Theroux makes almost every other travel writer seem insipid by comparison, though, given that the only travel books I have ever read are those by Theroux, Bruce Chatwin, and James Boswell, I am merely guessing here, and may only be saying this to be mean.

An American who had spent a good portion of his life in Britain, but almost exclusively in London, Theroux conceived of his remarkable feat not as a paltry "stunt"—like visiting every American saloon named the Dew Drop Inn—but as a means of traveling incognito in order to gather information behind enemy lines. As he puts it: "I sometimes felt like the prince in the old story, who because he distrusts everything he has been told and everything he has read, disguises himself in old clothes and, with a bag slung over his back, hikes the muddy roads talking to everyone and looking closely at things, to find out what his kingdom is really like." But I think he did it because it was faster than taking British Rail.

During his travels, Theroux visited an almost unbroken chain of comatose little towns, and seems to have encountered every bigoted, stupid, parsimonious, or boorish person in the United Kingdom, members of Parliament excluded. On a typical page he claims never to have stumbled upon a more dismal landscape, and then he makes the very same claim two pages later. An incurable sad sack but a truly wonderful writer, Theroux may have subconsciously set out on his journey with the sole purpose of demonstrating how a dyspeptic human being could make himself even more dyspeptic as long as he stayed on the hoof somewhere in the UK. Congenitally miserable myself, a writer whose sole source of income derives from shooting large, evil fish in a small, morally neutral barrel, this was my kind of reading. But reprising this sort of adventure did not seem like much fun. So throughout my jaunt across the Kingdom by the Sea, I generally stuck to public transportation.

This was probably a mistake. Trains in Britain are always late or breaking down or canceled for preposterous reasons like "unseasonably high winds in Cambridgeshire." You invariably have to check the schedule to make sure you're not on a train the day Chelsea is playing Arsenal, or Manchester United is playing anybody. Buses will take you just about anywhere, but they take forever to do it. Nobody but nobody can provide decent directions anywhere because everybody in Great Britain lives in his or her car and has forgotten how to calculate distances. The British Empire was built by coarse, heartless men who didn't mind walking great distances; at the Battle of Oudenarde in 1708, Marlborough (the very first Churchill) persuaded his already exhausted army to march another fifty miles in just sixty-five hours. Hundreds of infantrymen died or fell by the wayside, but the battle was ultimately won not by cannons or cavalry or even by unalloyed courage but by the insuperable force of naked, unmitigated pedestrianism.

But the days of imperial ambulatory glory are over. Today's average Briton has trouble walking to the refrigerator without having a seizure. I am not suggesting that this in itself caused the British Empire to collapse—Adolf Hitler, Gamal Nasser, and Mahatma Gandhi certainly had something to do with it—but it was certainly instrumental in the empire's decline.

Public transportation in Scotland is particularly cumbersome. In Edinburgh, widely considered to be the most beautiful city in Europe by people who have never been to Paris, there are two competing bus services. As a result, the unsuspecting traveler not only has to stand on a corner waiting for the right bus while a surprise mid-afternoon typhoon threatens to sweep him into the North Sea, but he has to make sure he is dealing with the right bus company. This is baffling to the innocents aboard who have purchased one company's day pass and then have to pony up an additional fare because they boarded the wrong conveyance. This is no way to run a tourist trap. On a personal note, I prefer funky Glasgow, which is both down-at-the-heels and up-and-coming, which has a much younger population, and which has more nightlife. Edinburgh is dainty and smug, like San Francisco; Glasgow is gritty and volcanic, like New York. Edinburgh is teeming with

American tourists who revel in its manicured tweeness; Glasgow is anything but twee. I know this is heresy, but I'll say it again: I prefer Glasgow.

There are other minor glitches in the Scottish public transportation cosmos. One day I took the train to Inverness, a beautiful city that sits on a lovely bay in northern Scotland. I was on my way to Culloden Moor, where Bonnie Prince Charlie's ragtag Highlander army was ripped to shreds in April 1746. After the battle, kilts and tartans were banned by the English government, though they later made a comeback as a staple of British pornography. To get to Culloden Moor, I walked to the Inverness bus terminal and climbed aboard a vehicle headed to Culloden, only to find that the bus to Culloden doesn't go to Culloden Moor. When I asked if the bus went anywhere *near* Culloden Moor, the bus driver told me that the trek would be interminable. It was in fact a two-mile walk atop a lovely hill with a glorious view of the harbor. Much of the way I walked backward just so I could take in the astonishing panorama. In fact, the only thing that is *not* glorious in this remarkable stretch of an unimaginably beautiful country is the dank swamp where Bonnie Prince Charlie elected to make his last stand against the Duke of Cumberland, the brute who henceforth was known as the Butcher.

I have never been a battlefields buff. Americans, enthralled by quasi-Homeric middlebrow epics like *Gone with the Wind* and *Cold Mountain,* are always dragging their incensed, exasperated children to killing grounds like Bull Run and Vicksburg, but the appeal is lost on me. Gettysburg is cluttered with so many monuments that it is impossible to visualize what the battlefield must have looked like the day the

Confederacy's fate was sealed by George Pickett's suicidal charge. If you hang around long enough, you do get the impression that the Johnny Rebs ceded the best terrain to the enemy and that Pickett's mad dash across a barren, unprotected field was a very bad idea. But the Confederate States of America were filled with bad ideas; the Civil War itself was a bad idea. The problem with "this hallowed ground" is that the monuments and educational kiosks and gift shops obscure the primordial savagery of the entire enterprise.

Gettysburg is also teeming with liquored-up reenactment buffs who have persuaded themselves that being a veteran of a re-creation of the events that transpired on Missionary Ridge or Shiloh is somehow akin to being a veteran of the real thing. This is like an ugly woman dressing up in a garter belt and mesh stockings and expecting everyone to mistake her for Marilyn Monroe. I despise Civil War buffs, with their endless prattle about the Louisiana Fusiliers and the Michigan Fifth Engineers. I abhor Civil War books and movies that somehow create the impression that the Lost Cause was in any sense *gallant*. I just generally hate anything to do with the Civil War.

Culloden Moor is a breath of fresh air for the carnage buff. It is a small, gloomy field with a few flags flapping in the breeze. The battlefield, revamped in 1980, today looks pretty much the same as it did on April 16, 1746, when the English forces, assisted by their enthusiastic Scottish allies, cut the Highlanders to ribbons. Like the Little Big Horn, the moor was a topographically injudicious site for making a last stand, unless you went into the battle with the full expectation that you were going to lose. There are no boulders to hide behind, no trees to mitigate the devastating effects of artillery. Whoever decided to duke it out here was an idiot.

Bonnie Prince Charlie was the idiot in question. Brought up in France without any military experience whatsoever, the twenty-four-year-old grandson of the deposed James II landed on a tiny island in the Hebrides in July 1745 determined to raise an army, invade England, reestablish a Catholic suzerainty, and drink the country dry. This, like Gettysburg, was a terrible idea. The English public had made it clear over the past two centuries that they did not want a Catholic king; they didn't care how bonny he was. And the Highlanders who rallied to the pretender's cause were loathed by forward-looking Scots who wanted this whole Catholics-versus-Protestants fiasco to come to an end so they could invent the modern world. (Personally, I am not persuaded that the Scots invented the modern world, any more than I am convinced that the Irish saved it. But it was certainly not the Mexicans.)

Nurtured on Robert Louis Stevenson's rousing *Kidnapped* and force-fed legends about Flora Macdonald, who helped smuggle the interloper out of Scotland after the debacle at Culloden without ever getting so much as a thank-you note in return, I expected to turn up at the Information Center and be fed a truckload of fanciful tripe about the dashing but doomed pretender to the throne. (At both the Museum of the Confederacy and the rebel White House in Richmond, Virginia, the pious tour guides try to make Jefferson Davis seem like a Dixie Priam, while pretending that the Confederacy in some labyrinthine way paved the way for the freeing of the slaves.)

But the short film that introduces visitors to the events that transpired at Culloden Moor minces no words in depicting Bonnie Prince Charlie as a simpleton. This certainly does not diminish the hideous savagery of the Duke of Cumberland, who on the eve of the engagement distributed a forged document stating that the Scots would show no quarter after the battle, thus justifying the Redcoats' slaughter of the wounded the following morning. But the film makes it clear that the Bonnie Prince's quest was even worse than quixotic, a prat's benighted escapade that cost thousands of lives and engulfed an entire nation in decades of misery and humiliation. So one comes away from Culloden Moor not with any Sir Walter Scottian sense of derring-do and romance, but merely sheer despair at the sublime stupidity of human beings.

And then you have to walk back to Inverness.

CITIZENS OF COUNTRIES THAT DEPEND HEAVILY ON TOURISM are undoubtedly fatigued by visitors' fetishistic obsession with cathedrals, tors, tumuli, standing stones, and killing fields. Scotland is a vibrant, modern nation with a highly distinctive culture, so it literally must drive Scotsmen mad that the only things tourists care about are inland sea monsters of dubious genetic provenance and locales where unspeakable things happened hundreds and in some cases thousands of years ago. But tourism is a massive industry in Scotland, so the locals have no one to blame but themselves for so energetically marketing their copious mythological wares.

Their main market is, of course, Americans. Americans have an insatiable appetite for anything that smacks of romance or reeks of tradition, having little of their own. If you want to know how Americans feel about preserving monuments, just remember that the original Waldorf-Astoria was not yet seventy years old when it was torn down to make way for the Empire State Building. Ben Franklin's house in Colonial Philadelphia is long gone; Betsy Ross's flag is a replacement. Almost no Federal Era structures remain in New York, and Colonial Williamsburg is a shameless con job filled with eighteenth-century buildings that the Rockefellers threw up in the 1920s. Americans do not want the weight of the past on their shoulders, so they gut everything. America has no truly ancient mythology; the deep historical past belongs to the Sioux and the Apaches, who were dispossessed and humiliated in their native land after the settlers got them tanked up on fire water. I am sorry that things have to be this way, but they are.

I DON'T MEAN TO LEAVE THE IMPRESSION THAT I SPENT ALL my time in the north country mired in the halcyon days of yore. I attended two concerts at the Royal Concert Hall in Glasgow. I saw a play in Edinburgh. I conducted an informal poll to see if it was true that Sean Connery was referred to in these parts as Big Tam. I visited a lot of pubs and restaurants and spent plenty of time chatting with the living rather than communing with the dead.

I also made several trips to Aberdeen, the City of Granite, which is like no other city I have ever been to, in part because it is made of granite. Aberdeen should be on every art lover's itinerary because the municipal museum jubilantly showcases Sir Edwin Landseer's *Flood in the Highlands,* quite possibly the worst painting in the world. Inundated with doomed tykes, forlorn patriarchs, bereft maidens, puzzled dogs, and characteristically oblivious farm animals, *Flood in the Highlands* is revoltingly mawkish, preposterously sentimental, and unbelievably grim, embodying in a single canvas all of the flatulent piety that makes Victorian painting such a treat for the *connoisseur de merde*. Landseer, who lived to be seventy-one, painted many bad paintings, but never again would he get things as completely out of kilter as he did here. Even by the standards of cruddy Highland paintings, this tasty little item is a doozy; Landseer had outdone himself.

Not everything in this cold, impersonal city is baleful. Just a stone's throw from the city center, which features a massive statue of William Wallace and a pair of glorious Edwardian public restrooms, stands a large group of tiny buildings arrayed in the form of a crescent. These too were made of granite. I was struck speechless by their grace, beauty, and ingenuity, so much so that I did not realize for quite some time that the unit constituted a Scottish housing project. Crescents are among the most remarkable architectural delights of Great Britain, and they pop up everywhere: Bath, Battersea, Aberdeen. A friend told me that one of the houses in the somewhat downscale crescent a few yards from King's Cross train station used to be a crack house. I suspected that the crack dealers were named Mr. and Mrs. Smackbotty, and that their dainty little home was christened Merlin's Ketch. I have never seen a crescent anywhere in America, which is almost entirely rectangular; they would certainly make grid-like Indianapolis more alluring. Crescents are my favorite architectural feature in Great Britain, rivaled only by closes.

If Baltimore only had a few closes, or even a couple of half-decent culs-de-sac, thrill-starved tourists would have something else to visit besides the crowded aquarium and overpraised baseball stadium, and house prices would go through the roof.

In short, I did not limit my visit to the obvious things one seeks out in Scotland. I stopped by some harrowing pubs. I visited a tattoo parlor. I was entertained by a homegrown stand-up comic, though I couldn't understand a word this Caledonian Robin Williams was saying. But no tourist worth his salt would dream of visiting Scotland without taking in Cawdor Castle, Loch Ness, Urquart Castle, Bannockburn, the Wallace Memorial, Stirling Bridge, and Culloden Moor. It would be like visiting Paris and skipping the Eiffel Tower; like visiting Gary, Indiana, and not dropping by Michael Jackson's house. On the sightseeing count, I failed only once; because I gave up drinking twenty years ago, I never bothered to visit any of Scotland's famous distilleries. Americans who spend a lot of time in renowned Scottish distilleries get so plastered they think they've not only seen the Loch Ness monster, but slept with it.

I have little to say on the Loch Ness score, other than that it's hard to get to. I visited the famous lake in the early nineties when my children were still quite small, but did not enjoy the seventy-two-hour, 120-mile trip from Huntley, 40 miles from Aberdeen, as we got stuck behind a Dutch VW bus and could not find the one place in northern Scotland where the road is wide enough to allow you to overtake. My children to this day honestly believe that they sighted the monster that afternoon, having spotted a huge, slimy green beast right around tea time, but I think it was a fat German tourist in the middle of a long overdue *wanderjahr*. Urquart Castle, poised in brooding splendor at the edge of the loch, is very nice indeed, as ruins go: the Scottish bookend to England's majestic Tintern Abbey. I was surprised to learn that the castle was destroyed not by Henry VIII or Edward I, but by Robert the Bruce, who did not want it used against him by Scots who were loyal to the English crown. Bruce himself had once been loyal to the crown, but only while the cruel, obsessive, bloodthirsty Edward Longshanks was still alive. Once word got out that Edward II's irrepressible lover, Piers Gaveston, had turned up at the king's nuptials decked out in the queen's jewels, the Bruce did an abrupt about-face, realizing that this was an Edward he could put a whipping on.

Scotland abounds with even more dubious mythology than its neighbor and frequent master to the south. Museums are chockablock with such objects as an enormous sword that probably did not belong to William Wallace, and a mummified heart that almost certainly never beat in the breast of Robert the Bruce. Saint Andrew's bones, once thought to be in the Holy Land, are now believed to be safely back home, personally delivered by an otherwise obscure angel, and King Duncan, allegedly murdered by Macbeth, is reputed to be buried under a filling station in Inverness, though the historical record indicates that he died in an entirely different part of the country, and was not murdered. Shakespeare, like Mel Gibson, played fast and loose with the facts, but was better with dialogue. For similar reasons, I doubt very much that it was the ghost of Banquo who stole my knapsack at Cawdor Castle, as Macbeth has nothing to do with the existing structure, and may well have been Thane of an entirely different Cawdor. There was no sign of blood anywhere in the castle, nor any special facilities associated with Lady Macbeth's compulsive ablutions. Cawdor Castle was a dud.

AFTER READING *THE KINGDOM BY THE SEA,* I DECIDED THAT my trip must also involve some sort of indisputably unique undertaking. But I didn't want the "stunt" to take up the entire book; I wanted to do something no one else had ever done before, but something that I could polish off quickly. My first thought was to spend a day examining all four copies of the Magna Carta. If I got to Salisbury Cathedral early in the morning, then doubled back to the British Library in London, where two copies are lodged, and then hotfooted it up to Lincoln, I would have eyeballed all four copies of the document that completely changed the world, and done it in a single day. But it seemed pointless and frivolous to rush through Lincoln and Salisbury, both of which are compelling cities, and besides, I didn't think anyone would be very impressed by this ploy. Next I considered visiting all the places where the kings of England had died violent deaths, but this would have taken months and required a side trip to Chaluz, the small town in Normandy where Richard the Lion-Hearted was felled by an archer's dart. Moreover, no one knows where King Arthur died, much less if he ever existed, and the precise site of Boadicea's alleged suicide is equally uncertain. The time may come when I am addled enough to believe that the ferocious warrior princess is entombed beneath a train platform in northeastern London, but that time has definitely not come yet.

Another idea was to visit the localities where assorted famous rock stars had perished long before their time, but I could never decide whether mumbling a prayer at the grave of the drummer from Led Zeppelin was worth as much of an effort as taking a snapshot of Brian Jones's house in Cheltenham. As I did briefly chat with the lead guitarist from the Animals after that rousing concert in Glasgow, and as he died several months later, it seemed that he had inadvertently given me a head start on the project. But I could never beguile myself into thinking that visiting the tomb of the lead guitarist from the Animals was on the same level, stuntwise, as visiting the grave of the man who founded the Rolling Stones, or, for that matter, the Muswell Hill semidetached where Ray Davies grew up. Quickly, the project fell by the wayside.

For various reasons, other projects were deep-sixed. Attending a football game in every major British city while wearing the colors of the team's most hated rivals seemed like a promising idea at first, but I am neither a brave nor a fool-hardy man, and on closer inspection it was hard to see what I would learn from this experience that I did not already know. I did try hiking the Cotswold Way blindfolded one day just to see how far I would get, but the infernal racket from the stroppy sheep outside Winchcombe gave me a headache. The sheep at the side of the trail would start bleating or braying— I never did find out which—and then the sheep half a mile up the trail would get into the act, and before long every mam-mal, bird, and reptile from Postlip Hall to Lacock Abbey knew I was coming. It was yet another case where Mother Nature, for reasons I can only suspect, had thrown up an insurmountable object in my path. So I threw in the towel.

I had just about given up hope of pulling off any truly memorable stunt when I happened to learn that the four quarters of William Wallace's desecrated corpse had been put on display in Berwick, Perth, Stirling, and Newcastle. I came into possession of this handy tidbit of information during one of my many chats about Wallace with the redheaded league to the north. Several people expressed outrage that Mel Gibson had left out the really juicy parts (think Peter Abelard), but I suspect that Gibson wanted a PG rating and didn't think that having the crown jewels sliced off on camera would help his career, even if he used a pelvic region stunt double. I would have thought the Scots would have been overjoyed that someone from Down Under had gone to such lengths to immortalize the nation's premier iconic figure, but instead people directed me to Web sites deploring all the factual errors in the film. (Wallace was not poor; he was not particularly friendly with Robert the Bruce; he did not invent the relatively ancient tactic of using spears to disembowel onrushing cavalry; he did not give up the ghost while Edward Longshanks was on his deathbed; he was not Australian.) The Scots sure drive a hard bargain.

While traveling in this highly idiosyncratic country, it became clear to me that the Scots did not like the English. A young man I had known as a stripling in Tarrytown had moved to Huntly after his American father's death. A terrific rugby player, and a very fine human being, he took me to Murrayfields Stadium to see the Scots get massacred by the French. It was one of the most bewildering experiences of my life: The Scots were all duded up in the Full Braveheart—painted faces, kilts, tams, flaming red wigs where flaming red hair was no longer tonsorially plausible—while the French had decked themselves out like the Three Musketeers. But everyone got along famously, sitting cheek by jowl in the stadium, sharing sandwiches, bellowing their national anthems. Of course, everyone was bombed out of their minds. After the game, the French and the Scots repaired to downtown pubs and traded tall tales. Two weeks later, I went to see Arsenal play Spurs at Highbury. No one sat cheek by jowl; no one shared any sandwiches; nobody invited any Spurs fans down to the pub for a postgame prandial.

My young friend, his hair redder than a Corsican sunset or a tart's knickers, explained that the French and the Scots liked one another immensely, united as they were by their hatred of the English. He asserted that before the Scots played the English each year, everyone went down to the pub and got plastered watching *Braveheart*. This seemed to be a tad self-defeating, as the Scots usually suffer the same fate as William Wallace when they meet the Limeys. The Scots may need a new theme movie. They definitely could use a new sport.

When my friend told me the story about Wallace's dismembered body being displayed in four different cities in the north (his head was stuck on a pike on London Bridge), I realized that I had already visited Berwick on the trip north from York, and had passed through both Stirling and Perth. This meant that in order to complete the Braveheart *tetrafecta*, I merely needed to stop off at Newcastle on my way back to London. So this was to be my lasting tourist achievement: I am the only person I know who has visited all four cities where the remains of William Wallace's body were displayed as a warning to Caledonian dissidents. This is a lot easier than walking around England or visiting the grave of every rock star who died before his time. As feats go, it is not especially Herculean, but I am not a Herculean traveler.

GEORGE SANTAYANA ONCE DECLARED THAT THOSE WHO cannot remember the past are condemned to repeat it. It is, to my knowledge, the only thing he is remembered for. I'm not sure he should even be remembered for that. The dictum is reminiscent of Oscar Wilde, forever given to semi-oracular pronouncements that on first blush seem to possess dazzling originality and wisdom, but that ultimately prove to be stupid. For example, it is not true that the only thing worse than being talked about is not being talked about; there are a million things worse than being talked about, like getting sent to Reading Gaol for two years and seeing your career destroyed.

What I find particularly interesting about Santayana's comment is that even if you do remember the past you are condemned to repeat it, because the present is nothing more than a serial reenactment of a microscopic number of possible pasts. Margaret Thatcher knew that she would ultimately be stabbed in the back and thrown out of office by a weary and in some ways ungrateful nation: Marlborough had been sent packing by an ungrateful nation, as had Pitt the Elder, so why shouldn't it happen to her? Thatcher was not surprised that she got stabbed in the back; she was merely surprised by the number of knives and the élan with which they were inserted. You can study history all you want, but sooner or later, you are going to meet your Waterloo. You merely hope that when you meet your Waterloo, you are vanquished by someone somewhat flashier than John Major.

Unlike most of my compatriots, I have always been obsessed with history, and particularly European history. This has long been a source of dismay for my wife, who cannot tell Marston Moor from Bosworth, but who has many other fine qualities. Her general disregard for British history is not surprising: Most Brits view the study of history as drudgery, because there is far too much of it. They cannot keep the Georges straight; they are even worse with the Ethelreds; they cannot tell you what the Corn Laws entailed; they have no idea what the Magna Carta actually says. (It says that the king can no longer run roughshod over everyone else's rights, as this is the prerogative of the nobility.) History is something that people in Britain keep locked up like the good silverware, and then when they pull it out, they can't remember which utensil goes where.

Yet, even though I am fascinated by British history, there is only so much that even I can take. By the end of my week in Scotland, I did not want to hear another word about William Wallace or Bonnie Prince Charlie, and I had certainly had my fill of Robert the Bruce. Much like Robert Lee in Virginia, Robert the Bruce turned up everywhere. There wasn't a village where he hadn't bedded down, a pub where he hadn't hoisted a few, a barnyard where he hadn't hidden from the Hammer of the Scots.

And those were merely the unofficial sightings. There was also a huge statue honoring his legendary victory over the English at Bannockburn, though the bus from Inverness to

Bannockburn doesn't actually take you to the site of the battle, because the battle was not fought in what is now Bannockburn. The statue is very impressive, but its placement is not: It sits in an educational center adjacent to a generic housing development. I felt that I owed it to both the Bruce and his nation to visit the monument, as I was a fan of the Philadelphia Eagles, Phillies, Flyers, and 76ers, perennial losers from back home, and found his ability to haul himself off the canvas and stagger back into the ring despite one murderous shellacking after another vaguely inspiring. Of course, it only took the Bruce around twenty years to win Scotland's freedom; the Eagles have never won the Super Bowl.

The central myth about Robert the Bruce involves his epiphany in a cave on an island off the coast of Scotland. Here he was so emboldened by the sight of an indomitable spider climbing up the wall, and falling back down, then climbing back up six times in succession until he achieved his goal, that he returned to his native land, raised the red flag of rebellion, and threw the English out for the next four hundred years. (The Bruce, not the spider.) I subsequently learned in reading through Magnus Magnusson's *Scotland: The Story of a Nation* that the tale is apocryphal; that it was actually a man named James Douglas who watched the spider climb the wall, not six but twelve times, and that Douglas then recounted the tale to Robert the Bruce, who took it to heart.

Why Robert the Bruce would be inspired by somebody else's ditsy tale about an industrious arachnid is beyond me, but this was, after all, the fourteenth century, when good epiphanies were hard to come by. In fact, even this version of the tale may be cooked up, as is the persistent rumor that the

Bruce may have treasonously fought alongside Edward Longshanks at the pivotal Battle of Falkirk. Or that he almost captured Wallace after that battle. Or that he was somehow
involved in Wallace's capture outside Glasgow, after which
Braveheart was sent to London to be tortured to death. Or, for
that matter, that he ever met William Wallace. Many of these
tales were devised by a fifteenth-century historian named
Blind Harry, who was probably not blind and may not have
been named Harry.

By the close of my visit to Scotland, I'd had it up to here
with Robert the Bruce. I had spent part of my trip with
friends in Huntly, and folks up there simply would not shut
up about Robert the Bruce. Huntly is a quaint village about
forty miles from Aberdeen, and is located in the Gordon
District. It is best known for its medieval castle, which Mary,
Queen of Scots almost visited, but begged off at the last
minute as she feared treachery on the part of its current occupant, a nobleman known as the Cock of the North. My son,
named Gordon, enjoyed vacationing in the town when he was
seven, as every building was named the Gordon Arms or the
Gordon Hotel or the Gordon Cafe. He even paid a visit to the
Gordon District Hospital after having his head smashed in
while playing miniature golf.

Huntly is the kind of place that adults love but that children despise, as there is nothing to do but grow a Mohawk, do
drugs, dress up like Eminem, or all of the above. The hills that
surround it turn purple in the summer when the heather is in
full flower, but Scottish adolescents are not impressed, nor
would Eminem be. One glorious afternoon I spent four hours
climbing up and down the hill directly across from my friend's

house, hoping to fulfill a lifelong dream of sweeping through the heather like Paul McCartney in "Mull of Kintyre." But I had only covered about thirty-five yards when I recalled Billy Connolly's prescient observation that it is not physically possible to "sweep" through the heather, as the heather will rip your legs to pieces. (It would be somewhat easier to sweep through the gorse, amble 'cross the moors, or clamber o'er the tussocks.) In the end, I swept *past* the heather, humming "The Long and Winding Road" all the while.

A few nights later, in a glum pub filled with men so old they may have been with Robert the Bruce at Bannockburn, I looked up and noticed that the video of "Mull of Kintyre" was playing on the television set above the bar. Nobody seemed to object. In 1297, Edward I, the aforementioned Hammer of the Scots, had laid waste to Scotland, imposing an alien culture on a people that had done nothing to merit such depravity. Gazing up at Paul McCartney and Linda Eastman cavorting with the bagpipe players on the beach, I found it hard to see how anything had changed.

Much of my time in Huntly was spent visiting the countryside, which was possible because it did not rain the entire week. In fact, it was sunny; I may be the only tourist to ever spend a week in northern Scotland in the winter and come back with a tan. I also spent a good deal of time marveling at highlight films of a superb New Zealand rugby player whose skills simply took my breath away, even though I think rugby is stupid. And, of course, we all chatted endlessly about Mel Gibson's failures as a historian, while gobbling up mammoth steaks and epic portions of haggis.

Alas, our conversations inevitably turned to Robert the Bruce. It just so happens that Battle Hill, which stands directly behind my friend's house, is the site of one of the Bruce's many defeats. After the battle, the Bruce was nursed back to health in nearby Huntly Castle, which is now an upscale hotel, restaurant, and conference center no longer associated with the Cock of the North. I was told that the peripatetic Bruce had also surfaced in a tiny village a few miles up the road. One night, my friend even floated a theory that when the Bruce beat one of his inimitable "hasty retreats" from Battle Hill, he may have staggered down her very driveway, which had not yet been built.

This was the moment when I decided to beat *my* hasty retreat. Packing my bags, I headed due south. In cosmopolitan Glasgow, I was sure, nobody would bend my ear about Robert the Bruce and his eensy-weensy spider.

I could not have been more wrong. The next morning, I found myself in Glasgow's central square. The square is filled with statues honoring famous Scots—David Hume, James Watt, Walter Scott—but the pièces de résistance are mounted statues of the young Queen Victoria and Albert, her beloved Prince Consort, who died young and unloved, primarily because he was German and the English weren't. Seeking to confirm my aforementioned theory that nobody in Britain really knows much about their own history, I began asking passersby if they could tell me who was mounted on the mighty steeds. I got some pretty startling answers—Mary, Queen of Scots, Elizabeth II, the Princess Alexandra, Margaret, the Maid of Norway (Wrong! She died at the age of eight), but not one of the fifty people I polled came close to giving me the correct answer. Including a tour guide.

Just then two elderly Englishwomen buttonholed me. Recognizing my accent, a woman who introduced herself as Mary Mooney told me an astounding tale about working in Beverly Hills as Jimmy Durante's maid back in the 1940s. (For the younger members of the audience, Jimmy Durante was an alarmingly unattractive Depression Era comedian with a huge schnozz whose signature tune was the somewhat-less-than-immortal "Inka-dinka-doo.") The woman's *séjour* at his Beverly Hills home was, to my knowledge, the only recorded example of an explicitly Caledonian cut to his jib. The marooned Maid of the Menial Moors now apprised me that she always carried a photograph of a prospective benefactor in her wallet and was convinced, for reasons she did not divulge, that if she could merely get his ear he would assuredly solve all her problems with the Immigration and Naturalization Services. Mary was pretty long in the tooth to be thinking about a twilight career in the domestic services industry, but I didn't tell her that, as this was no way to treat a cleaning lady. Eventually, I said that I would see what I could do and asked who the man was. She immediately produced a sleek, well-preserved newspaper clipping that proved to be a photo of Donald Trump.

I hold no brief for Donald Trump, a thoroughly objectionable human being. Still, because of the imploring look in the woman's eyes, I would have been willing to dash off a short letter to the self-promoting real estate baron and casino operator, asking if he could find it in himself to lend this poor soul a hand. But then I asked Mrs. Mooney where she lived, and she pronounced the fatal words, explaining that while she was originally from England, she was now living in a small cottage on the outskirts of Glasgow where Robert the Bruce had once spent the night.

"That cuts it, lady," I told her, gathering up my belongings without even giving her a chance to rev up the spider story. "I've had all I can take of the Bruce; *you* get in contact with the Donald."

10

Hadrian's Wall—and Step on It!

One should never buy shoes in a foreign country. For starters, American feet are shaped differently than English feet, and American colors are different from English colors. So is our fashion sense; in America, brown is not considered a festive hue, and grown men who wear plaid pants anywhere but the fairway are regularly mowed down by thugs manning canary yellow Hummers. It is all right to buy socks and underwear while abroad, and in an emergency it is perfectly acceptable to purchase trousers, shirts, and sweaters. But one should never, ever buy shoes.

It had always been a dream of mine to visit Hadrian's Wall. In retrospect I should have worn better footwear. I had arrived in London several weeks earlier wearing dress shoes that were inappropriate for traveling, and immediately realized that I needed a pair of serviceable hiking boots. One desultory morning, as I was gravitating toward Green Park, I spotted a pair of cobalt blue boots that were exactly what I wanted. Inside the front door stood five young men. I tried opening the door, but it was locked. The manager of the shop, making no attempt to mask his pique, opened the portal about the width of a tubercular partridge and advised me to return in thirty minutes, as the staff was busy at the moment receiving "additional training."

I returned to the shop at the appointed time and was ushered into the store by the same man. He was about thirty, bespectacled, persnickety, a bit on the cadaverous side. I pointed out the boots I wanted and told him my size. He came back two minutes later with a pair of lurid green boots. I explained that I wanted the boots in blue, the ones in the window, the ones I had just finished showing him. He said that the particular model in question did not come in blue in my size. This was inconceivable. I didn't mind being told that the blue size 47s had run out, but resented being told that the manufacturer, a respectable Australian company, adhered to a blue color scheme all the way up to size 43, and then inexplicably switched to green. It beggared speech; it flew in the very face of all I believed about shodding; it violated the cobbler's code. A company like that simply would not last.

My anger was both professional and personal; I had never accepted being lied to by shoe salesmen; having plied my trade in the footwear business as a boy, I had never once fibbed, much less dissembled, about styles, colors, price, availability, or how good the various models looked on the customer's feet. To do so would have been a breach of the unwritten statutes of podiatric ethics, giving way to a subtle yet pernicious duplicity that in time could eat away at the very fabric of society. Furious, I told the man that at future confabs where "additional staff training" was provided, the store might consider telling employees that people who wanted blue shoes didn't like being manipulated into buying green ones.

My interlocutor now got a bit shirty, wearily remarking that the items he was offering were exactly the same model, implicitly suggesting that color did not matter. All in, I then reminded him, lest he had forgotten, that green boots were objectionable to baby boomers, because they reminded us of Vietnam, Algeria, and Suez. Besides, green was a revolting color. I could see that I had struck home; a Gen Xer par excellence, he knew that green was in fact a deplorable color for footwear, and that his generation only wore it to be *snarky*. I then demanded that Irony Boy provide me with the name and address of the manufacturer, vowing by the loins of Hengist that should I determine that his assertions about the company's coloring code were in error, I would return and rain not only fire and brimstone but rank contumely upon his head. Oh yes, if I found out that he was lying, there would be hell to pay—and let Satan take the hindermost!

I never did get around to contacting the manufacturer, as that is the sort of thing my wife does, and she was back in the United States, knitting somber scarves. Instead, two days later I bought a very nice pair of hiking boots that were similar in both style and color to the model I really wanted, but just slightly darker. Alas, the shoes were accursed. They gave me blisters, bunions, and corns from the first day I put them on, they never fit right no matter what socks I wore, and they didn't even look that good. This unfortunate purchase, which set me back roughly seventy pounds, cast an orthopedic cloud over the remainder of my trip.

One brisk morning a few weeks later I slipped on the misbegotten boots and headed out to inspect the North Yorkshire moors. I had spent three delightful days in the city of York, whose magnificent cathedral I had longed to visit for many years. Now I finally got to hear Evensong in the magnificent cathedral and to physically examine the site of Constantine's ascension to power (well, not really; a deaconess in the bowels of the structure admitted that the actual site was concealed behind a wall because of unrelated plumbing issues).

York also had a very fine Mexican bistro.

Was my visit an unalloyed pleasure? It was not. While in York, I got more than my fill of the Plantagenet industry cooked up by Josephine Tey and the Northern Yorkshire Tourism Bureau: prisons, bookstores, museums, pubs. The locals, needless to say, absolved Richard III of responsibility for the murder of the little princes, insisting that it was a frame job by Henry VII and William Shakespeare, possibly with assistance from medieval prototypes of the CIA, the KGB, the Cosa Nostra, powerful Texas oilmen, the Bavarian Illuminati, the International Jewish conspiracy, or the Trilateral Commission. They rattled on and on about the king's physique, insisting that while Richard Crouchback may have had a slight, slight deformity, he was certainly no kin of Quasimodo, and was indisputably an excellent dancer. Even the wicked Tudors, gifted dancers in their own right, would concede *that*. The Yorkish seemed to believe that because the depraved king was an excellent dancer, he could not possibly have butchered his innocent nephews, the rightful heirs to the throne, as those who were light on their feet did not go in for that sort of thing. But Al Capone and Henry VIII were also excellent dancers, and they murdered everyone from crooked cops to Cistercian monks to slow-paying bootleggers to tarts with three breasts. There is not the slightest doubt in my mind that Richard III killed the little princes; my personal conspiracy theory is that Richard III was not, in fact, an excellent dancer, but hired an impersonator to take his place on the ballroom floor so that he could slip away to the Tower of London and slit his nephews' throats while everyone mistakenly believed he was performing one of his vaunted gavottes.

Wearying of this late medieval balderdash, I flagged down a bus bound for the nearby moors. Never a huge fan of crags and declivities, I only dragged myself out to the moors because my recently deceased father was always going on and on about them, and I thought it would be a nice gesture to take a gander. Having never visited these shores, my father misidentified the Yorkshire moors as the setting for *The Hound of the Baskervilles*, when in fact the famous Sherlock Holmes tale takes place in Devon, not far from the church where Carver Doone shot Lorna. The man sitting next to me on the bus was an elderly, retired grave digger on his way home to Whitby, whose brooding castle ruins had inspired Bram Stoker to write *Dracula*. Introducing himself as Jim, he discussed his plans to cook himself a tasty fox stew with the leeks he had just purchased in town. He did not say where the fox came from. Jim had an almost impenetrable accent, and

could easily have played a canny rogue in a *Masterpiece Theater* presentation of *The Mayor of Casterbridge,* except that
Hardy's novel is set in Dorset. He was under the impression
that Philadelphia was in California—if only!—and lamented
that the grave-digging trade was not what it once was. I asked
him why he had retired from the business and he said that a
couple of years earlier he'd had a heart attack while digging
another man's final resting place.

"That was convenient," I suggested.

"No, it wasn't," he replied. "I was miles from the hospital
and all by myself out there. And it was hot. It was so hot."

"No, I mean it was convenient that you were standing in a
grave when you had your heart attack," I explained. "If you'd
died, you wouldn't have had to go very far."

He had no idea what I was talking about.

"It was another man's grave," he fired back. "I was digging
another man's grave. It wasn't my grave. But it was hot. It was
so bloody hot."

Jim thought that Philadelphia was in California.

The day I visited the moors, they appeared to be closed
due to rain. I jumped off the bus outside a pub, plunged into
the conveniently located wilderness, thrashed about in the
mud for a couple of hours, sank into a yawning abyss, and
wrecked my boots. The whole time I was walking on the
moors, where, if memory serves correctly, little Jane Eyre
very nearly met her fate, a group of senescent bikers followed closely in my wake, inexplicably blasting Johnny
Mathis's *Greatest Hits* on a portable boom box. Intermittently, American jet planes from a nearby military base
would rocket across the heavens, perhaps on a search-and-

destroy mission for Osama bin Laden, who may have been hiding in a nearby cave, as the entire area resembles Afghanistan. I kept trying to imagine what it would be like to get lost out here like the misbegotten Jane Eyre, though I would never have retreated to such a barren landscape, and certainly not because my heart swelled in my bosom over a bastard like Rochester.

Emerging from the coarse landscape, I staggered into a quaint tea shop but was told to leave my boots outside, as they were a mess. It seemed disingenuous and a bit cheeky for a tea shop located in the middle of the North Yorkshire moors to impose a no-muddy-footwear dress code, so I nixed the scones and finger sandwiches and grabbed the next bus back to York. Arriving at the hotel, I was told to leave my boots in the vestibule, where a manservant or maid would clean them. This was the first time anyone had ever offered to clean mud off my boots; it made me feel all chuffed and special, like the Earl of Tetley returning from a duel in the brackish mists of Islington. (I have always had a deep and abiding fear of bed-and-breakfasts, due to the latent menace of garrulous land-ladies who will not stop haranguing you about the long, vaunted history of the nearby woolen mill, but revel in the impersonality of hotels, where the staff is superficial and smarmy, but will clean the mud off your boots for a fiver.) Alas, alack, the mud never, ever came out of those boots; today, twenty-four months later, having endured snowstorms, monsoons, and full submersion in the flash floods that regularly sweep through my basement, the caked mud remains embedded in the thoroughly uncomfortable items. This is the worst pair of shoes I have ever owned; the only reason I do not chuck them into the trash or donate them to the Salvation Army is because they remind me of my wonderful trip to Great Britain and because I am unbelievably cheap.

SOMEONE ONCE SAID THAT TELEVISION IS NEVER MORE foolish than when it is trying to be intelligent. I feel the same way about American tourists. American tourists are never more annoying than when they attempt to masquerade as refined, sensitive, kindred spirits traipsing across the country-side and lilting meadows on a leisurely *wanderjahr,* rather than the concupiscent philistines they really are. For an American to stop and smell the roses, the coffee, or any com-bination thereof, is a repudiation of his national heritage. For an American to relax and take pleasure in small things—a sunset, a wee pot of tea and a bicky at Sally Slapcabbage's, eight seconds of uninterrupted sunshine—is to repudiate his birthright to behave like a hyperactive glutton. Americans are first and foremost consumers; like sharks, when they stop moving, pushing forward, buying things—they die. Obviously, sharks do not actually buy things, but my general drift is clear. Americans were not put on God's green earth to relax, reflect, dawdle, or ruminate. They were put on this earth to get their ass in gear, put the pedal to the metal, and buy stuff.

Unless you are the type of dyspeptic writer who sets out to meet every Grumpy Gus from Land's End to John o' Groats, the determined traveler can traverse most of Great Britain without encountering any real oafs. I was treated amiably by soccer hooligans in Manchester, truck drivers in Liverpool, and pub owners in Brixton. I was regaled with tall tales by retired firemen in Portsmouth, and treated to free drinks by academics in Oxford. I managed to spend six weeks in Britain and met only a handful of people I absolutely despised: a twittish journalist who moderated a panel in York and objected to my statement that you could not use Pink Floyd's *Dark Side of the Moon* in a serious radio broadcast without pissing off everybody who was not a stoner, and a limo driver who took me to Heathrow Airport eight months after 9/11 and spent the entire ride haranguing me about American insensitivity to the Muslim world, asserting that 90 percent of people in the Muslim world hated Americans.

"I think that figure might be a bit low," I cautioned him. "Why not just come out and admit that you hate all of us and we hate all of you. Honesty is the best policy."

He then apologized for being a bit disoriented; his wife had just given birth to twins, and he had not been sleeping much lately. He now proudly announced that he had named one of his sons Osama, which was a very common practice in the Arab world. I told him that it was a very common practice back where I came from to refrain from tipping people who had named one of their sons Osama eight months after 9/11. It was nothing personal; Americans were funny that way.

I had one other bad experience; it occurred the morning I set out for Hadrian's Wall. I rose early at the Master of Ballantrae Bed & Breakfast in Edinburgh, high-stepped it over to the Princes Street train station, and headed due south. Outside the station stands a colossal statue of Sir Walter Scott. I could not imagine anything like this in America; if the city fathers erected a statue in honor of Mark Twain, the spiritual father of modern American literature, activists would demand that it be torn down because Twain used the word *nigger* too often. It was inconceivable that anyone would bankroll a statue memorializing Henry James or Herman Melville or Edith Wharton or William Faulkner; if any statues were going up, they would have been in honor of John Grisham, Stephen King, or V. C. Andrews.

The train was bound for Carlisle, on the west coast of England, and this was where my luck ran out. Carlisle is a small, reasonably congenial city in northwestern England. It is of interest to the antiquities buff because it is home to the second-smallest cathedral in Britain and is located not terribly far from the region where Hadrian's Wall begins. Although the ancient Roman edifice is one of the true wonders of the ancient world, most Americans don't know anything about it. Once, upon my return to New York, I mentioned to a friend that I had seen Hadrian's Wall while I was in England. "Who was in it?" he asked, mistaking it for a fatuous West End musical. In the words of the immortal Johnny Carson, I kid you not.

Frequently misidentified as the official barrier between Scotland and England back in Roman times (the Great Wall of Caledonia, if you will), the roughly eighty-mile structure in fact sits some distance from the Scottish border. (The Antonine Wall is closer to Scotland, but less impressive, in far worse condition, and even more obscure.) Erected by the mighty Roman emperor Hadrian in the year 122 it was thrown up to keep out the thieving Scots and feisty Picts, but was never the official frontier between the dueling nations. Mostly, it served as a kind of customs check. Over the course of the centuries, large sections of the wall have been destroyed by marauders, farmers, hippies, and scavenging stonemasons.

But sizable fragments remain in reasonably intact condition. It had long been my ambition to lope along the wall in the footsteps of Hadrian, and now that I had no obligation to visit beloved Aunty Margaret, who was dead by this juncture, I hastened me hither to the magnificent edifice. Francis Bacon once said that he who hath both wife and children hath given hostages to fortune. In fact, what he hath given hostages to is tourism.

As noted, I visited Carlisle because it was reasonably close to the wall, because there were several intact remnants of the edifice nearby, and because I wanted to make a side trip to the second-smallest cathedral in Britain. But everyone I met in the frigid, uncooperative burgh was a pain in the ass. The jubilantly uninformative man working in the train station's ticket office had no idea how to get to the ancient structure. The bus drivers were clueless. The staff in the tourist bureau confirmed that there was a Hadrian's Wall bus line somewhere or other near the train station, but when I turned up at the designated street corner I discovered that the service only operated from May to September. The locals could not have been less interested.

"It's not around here," yawned a man in a butcher's shop.

"I've never been there," added a woman in a coffee shop, exuding the fierce pride of the townie who has made a pact with Satan to never go anywhere near anything local that might be of passing interest. I had, of course, crossed paths with these yokels before—the people who live down the street from the Tyrolean chapel in Selsley who have never bothered to wander inside to check out the windows by Dante Gabriel Rossetti and Ford Madox Brown; the South Kensington poseur who claims to have never visited Clapham Common.

They are the types of people who exhibit an almost exuberant pride in their own indifference, pouting rubes who would rather be gnawed on by famished hyenas than visit a majestic monument a scant fifty yards down the road. "It's all right for some to go gallivanting around Hadrian's bloody Wall," is their attitude. "But I've got to get to the co-op and stock up on Bovril." Mind you, I have lived in New York since 1976 and have never been anywhere near the Statue of Liberty.

Bus drivers are particularly unaccommodating in these situations. When you ask how to get to Hadrian's Wall, they act as if you've just asked them for directions to the Silk Road or the Trans-Indonesian Highway. Gleeful at the traveler's admitted ignorance of the lay of the land, they guard potentially useful data about bus routes the way Rumpelstiltskin conceals his name. They seem astounded that anyone would even be interested in visiting Hadrian's Wall when there is so much else to see in Carlisle, which does after all boast Britain's second-smallest cathedral. And they go out of their way to chide you in the studiously condescending way that is the stock-in-trade of the ill-tempered public servant, acting as if no one in the long and noble history of northern English public transportation had ever mentioned the Roman Empire before.

"Can't get to Hadrian's Wall on this line," they caw, as if you had just requested directions to Machu Picchu. "I only go as far as Linton Tweeds."

Consulting a map, I spotted a little town called Haltwhistle situated just about halfway between Carlise and Newcastle. From the looks of things, it was very close to a well-maintained fragment of the wall. I hopped on a train and made the short junket across the Pennines, spending the whole time looking out the window at the glorious countryside. England, like Scotland, is a country where it is absolutely pointless—and irreverent—to carry a book or newspaper because the views are so spectacular. You can always read *Bel Canto* or *The Tibetan Book of the Dead* when you are safely back home in your standard-issue suburban home; to waste time reading in Scotland, England, or Wales seems sacrilegious. (For the same reason, I never go to the movies while traveling, unless I am going to be away for a long, long time or required to do so for work. I once spent ninety-three minutes, forty-three seconds in a Soho screening room watching a David Spade movie; it was like checking into a Tuscan hospital for brain surgery while everyone else wandered off to the Uffizi.)

One often gets the sense in traveling across Great Britain that everyone has been dispatched directly from central casting to make your visit more enjoyable. The obsequious clerk. The fussy innkeeper. The demented soccer fan. The garrulous deacon. The plump stationmaster. Of course, part of the appeal of the English is their reassuring dowdiness. Americans can never pull this off. Americans, even ancient ones, are too much in the thrall of Marlon Brando, James Dean, Fran Drescher. Americans are obsessed with appearing to be cool long after this is possible, or even advisable. The British give it up by age thirty-five.

The station mistress in Haltwhistle looked like a character straight out of *Thomas the Tank Engine*. She was a full-sized, gregarious, middle-aged woman with electrifying red hair and a highly musical accent. She was shockingly friendly, and extraordinarily helpful.

"You can walk to the wall from here; it's about two miles," she explained. "But the best part of the wall is about seven miles away."

Seven miles was farther than I cared to walk, as I was carrying luggage. For that matter, two miles was too far to walk. I had a blister on my right foot by this point and was running out of energy. The station mistress volunteered to stow my luggage until I returned, but that still didn't solve the problem of getting to the wall.

"Are there any taxis around here?" I asked her. "I know that visiting Hadrian's Wall by taxi is a bit tacky, but I am after all an American."

The station mistress rang for a cab. It turned up about ten minutes later. The driver sped off to the wall and dropped me off at a suitably historic locale. He also gave me his phone number for the return trip, though as I had no cell phone of my own and there are no public phones on Hadrian's Wall itself, this was of no use to me.

In America, rural areas are never entered into casually. In the pits of our stomachs, we are always waiting for the toothless mountain men from *Deliverance* to show up. In reality, much of this terror is misinformed; these days one is unlikely to visit a rural swamp and cross paths with tooth-less mountain men, as most of them are serving in the state legislature or anchoring late-night programs on the Fox News Channel.

Britain is entirely different. It is a place where an American can simultaneously feel both out of place and completely at home, never needing to fear the escapades of promiscuous rustics. And because it was Good Friday, there was no one anywhere near the serpentine structure when I first glimpsed it. I had the whole thing to myself. Well, it was quite a wall. Parts of it had vanished; in some places, only small fragments had survived. But huge sections remained. Oh yes, it was a wall to be reckoned with, a history buff's delight. Without question, it was the best wall I had ever seen. But I didn't need to walk seven miles of it, as one got the idea pretty quickly. So I took a few photographs, reflected intently for perhaps ten seconds on the vanity of human wishes and the evanescence of fame, then hitchhiked back to Haltwhistle.

After a brief, convivial tête-à-tête with the affable station mistress, I boarded a train to Newcastle. I had been there only once, ten years earlier, on a trip to Aberdeen. I'd come north from Cheltenham with my family, and we had a seventy-five-minute layover in the town where Eric Burdon and the Animals had grown up. Depositing my own animals in a nearby restaurant, I slipped away to visit eight cathedrals, seventeen abbeys, and a couple dozen crypts. On my way back to the station, I spotted a shop called Transformations. It had frosted windows and a darkened door. I stepped inside and found myself in a nifty emporium filled with all manner of exotic costumes. The nun. The nurse. The schoolgirl. The dominatrix. The riding instructor. The French maid.

The outfits came in large sizes.

I turned around and asked the cashier, who appeared to be Pakistani, what a shop catering to well-heeled cross-dressers was doing in down-at-the-heels Newcastle.

"The manager will be back from lunch in thirty minutes," he replied, handing a gnarled customer a copy of *A Lesson for Laddy; or, Return to St. Trinian's.* "You'll have to ask him."

I would indeed, the next time I was in town and didn't have a train to catch. For the moment, I simply marveled at the experience. London was filled with shops such as Transformations, and many British cities boasted similar sex emporia of all sizes and descriptions. But grotty, working-class Newcastle didn't seem like the kind of place that could support a large, active population of men who liked to get dressed up as Chantal, the saucy maid who was not always *bonne*. A week later, I mentioned this incident to Scottish friends at dinnertime, expressing my astonishment that such a cosmopolitan enterprise could be found in a city as seemingly proletarian as Newcastle. The other diners found it an unusual and obstructive conversational gambit; they were keen to get back to our discussion of Robert the Bruce. Then an older man spoke up.

"The port in Newcastle is where all the ferries from Norway come in," he said. Then he went back to eating. So that was it! Transformations could never have made a go of it by catering to impoverished locals. But it could do a land-office business by purveying its wares to a steady influx of well-heeled Norwegian cross-dressers. *How could I have been so stupid?*

In reality, I never truly bought into that theory. But in the intervening period I hadn't had much time to develop more plausible ones, as I was busy getting on with my life. And so, a decade had passed. Now, determined to get to the bottom of this enigma, I put the shop at the top of the list on my Newcastle itinerary. But first I stopped off at the Parish Church of St. John the Baptist to attend a traditional Good Friday service. I arrived at the church doorstep precisely at three in the afternoon, the moment when Christ is reputed to have expired, but the door would not budge. This was annoying, as I could hear baleful singing emanating from inside. So I knocked. And knocked. And knocked again. Eventually, a sexton came to the door and said that there was a service going on, as it was Good Friday, and no tourists were needed. I said that I knew it was Good Friday, as I was a Catholic, and even though I was a lapsed one, I never missed religious services on Good Friday because I still held out a vague hope of someday returning to the One True Church and perhaps slipping into Paradise through the back door via a deathbed rapprochement with my savior, not unlike the Emperor Constantine.

The man let me in, grumbling all the while, then locked the door behind me. Now I was trapped. I had intended to participate in a typically British Good Friday service, but I had not been planning on a service that lasted two hours. Now there was nothing to do but gut it out. The service went on forever, somewhat longer than Christ's crucifixion. It was one of those lugubrious affairs where the first vestryman intoned the words "Jesu Christu," and then the second one repeated it, and then the rest of the congregation chimed in with "Jesu Christu," but then, just when you thought they were going to move on to "Agnus Dei" or "Dies Irae," and get some points on the lenten scoreboard, they went right back to "Jesu Christu." The hymns lasted an eternity. The sermon was interminable. There were abundant prayers for fallen comrades in Rwanda, Kosovo, West Ham. It simply would not end. I had carried my deadly mixture of omnivorous sightseeing and resurgent Christianity too far, and now I was paying the price. I could see that the sexton was enjoying all this; he kept his eyes riveted on me the whole time, prepared to intervene should I make a break for the doorway during Communion. I had no choice but to sit there and suffer in silence. Father, my Father, why *hadst* Thou forsaken me?

It took 120 minutes to reach the *"Eoi Eoi, lama sabachthani"* send-off, and as soon as the doors reopened I bolted into the sunlight like a bat out of hell. Now I was in the mood for a little sightseeing. Young people were always telling me that Newcastle was an exciting city, a city on the rebound, a city on the move. The physical evidence suggested otherwise. The downtown looked like a dump. The shops were grotty. The streets were filled with people who looked suspiciously like bums. Young people judge cities like Manchester and Newcastle by the amount of nightlife they have to offer, and are generally oblivious to how the cities look in the daytime. I am not. I count bums. And I was uncomfortable with the numbers I came up with.

Still, I was determined to spend a night there. Unfortunately, the downtown hotels were booked solid by legions of football fans who had stormed up from Everton to see their team annihilate Newcastle. In fact, sixty thousand of them were coming right down the street. They were in an ugly mood, breaking bottles, harassing shoppers, picking fights. I wondered how things would have turned out had they lost. This seemed like a good time to jump on the next train to anywhere. Consulting my trusty map, I noticed that ancient Durham was only twenty minutes away. So I bought a ticket and sped off to the site of England's oldest, most breathtaking cathedrals, but not before checking to see if Transformations was still a going concern. It was not; it was gone. The mystery of the Norwegian cross-dressers would not be solved today. If ever.

The train was filled with chanting, boozed-up Everton supporters; luckily, I was wearing the same color jacket as them, so I was in like Flynn. A woman sitting across from me volunteered that her brother lived in Las Vegas. If he looked anything like her—frowsy, cheap—I was hardly surprised. While I was traveling in Britain, people were always haranguing me with tales of daughters in northern Tennessee or nephews in western Florida or cousins in Reno and asking if I had ever been to any of these frightful places. I sometimes detected a peculiar type of gloating going on here; well, Mr. World Traveler, you've seen Tintern Abbey and York Cathedral, but I've been to Caleb's Funk Shack in Pascagoula. And I've seen Céline Dion at the MGM Grand. That's right; you have, and I haven't. But I can tell the difference between a fork and a spoon.

Beneath all this, there was something infuriatingly patronizing. When Americans travel abroad, they go out of their way to praise the finest points of their hosts' civilization. The English, by contrast, are fixated on the grotesque: the alligator wrestlers in Orlando, the Tennessee theme park dedicated to Dolly Parton. They are determined to invent their own America (a fun house), and anything that does not fit this template will be jettisoned. The last thing the British, laden down with tradition and history, want to see when they come to America are obvious signs of culture and intelligence. By contrast, Americans are uncomfortable with the idea that most inhabitants of the British Isles are dull, plodding, prejudiced, obvious, and unsophisticated. Americans want to believe that the average Brit wears a bowler and a school tie and maintains a stiff upper lip and has a certain dry sense of humor; they do

not want to be told that a good percentage of the British population are vulgar dimwits who care about nothing but shopping, alcohol, football, and Posh Spice's navel. Our concept of
Britain derives from Agatha Christie; the Brits' concept of
America derives from *Dallas.*

Nobody on the train to Everton was wearing a bowler hat.

Arriving in Durham, I hailed a taxi and asked the driver if
he could recommend a good bed-and-breakfast. The driver's
name was Pat. Bonded by a tenuous ethnic liaison, Pat
cheered me with the news that the students at the university
had all gone home for the Easter holidays, and thought I
might be able to rent one of their rooms. Then he had an even
better idea. He said I might be able to get a room at the nine-
hundred-year-old castle that stood directly across from the
cathedral.

Pat was right. Reporting to the tiny office in the gateway of
the castle, I asked if any rooms were available. The man in
charge said that all the units in the castle per se were rented,
but that he did have a room in the gatehouse tower, if I didn't
mind drafts and the ghost. I minded neither. The price was
twenty quid, breakfast included. I was beside myself with
glee. I attended yet another Good Friday service in the cathedral not a hundred yards from my bedroom; the music was
provided by a chipper but undertalented ensemble that
sounded like a Salvation Army band that had escaped from a
supper club production of *Major Barbara.* It *was,* in fact, the
Salvation Army band. The cathedral, as previously noted, was
one of the oldest in Britain, so I was not terribly surprised that
it contained the remains of Saint Cuthbert. That was another
fifteen minutes of sightseeing right there. Dinner at a local

Indian restaurant was divine; a German graduate student I encountered at the castle acted as my tour guide for the next twenty-four hours. This in itself was utterly unexpected; I had never previously met a German whose company I enjoyed, a situation I do not expect to improve when I finally break down and visit Berlin a few years hence. That night, I had immense trouble getting to sleep, transfixed as I was by the majestic cathedral just across the path. I could not believe my good fortune. I could not believe the view. I could not believe that I was out just twenty quid. I was very possibly the happiest man on the face of the earth.

Purists will object to the inherent vulgarity of this sort of madcap itinerary. Only a crass American would start the day in glorious Edinburgh, whip right through Carlisle without stopping by its remarkable cathedral, speed-visit Hadrian's Wall, make a quick jaunt through Newcastle, and wrap up the festivities in historic Durham. But I am a crass American, and rather enjoy being one. Britain is an economically sized nation that can be traversed quickly, and I for one see no reason to dawdle. As I have noted time and time again, my concept of tourism involves getting in and out quickly, taking in the sights and sounds with a commando-like precision, and then having a damn fine curry. I did not want this day to end; it had been a kind of miracle. But at three in the morning, I finally retired to my bed. The next day, I needed to check out Leeds, Nottingham, Sheffield, and, time permitting, Coventry. The culture vulture's work is never done.

Next visit, I'd bring more comfortable shoes.

11

Rule, Britannia

When my children were still very small, we spent an idyllic summer vacation in a tiny cottage in Brimscombe, which sits up the hill from Stroud, a stone's throw from the uncompromisingly twee Minchinhampton. The royal horsey set spends a good deal of their time in this region, and would not do so were the district not prodigiously equine. The cottage, it goes without saying, had a name—The Nook—and was owned by an elderly widow who lived in the adjacent Field House. The cottage was chockablock with heavy, oppressive furniture and was notable for its many oddities. For example, if you turned on the water in the kitchen, you would adversely affect the water pressure in the bathroom. This, perhaps, was not so very odd, though, as I have generally found when traveling in Britain, if you turn on the cold tap in Penzance, someone will almost certainly get an electrical shock in Bury Saint Edmunds.

There were all sorts of "rules" and "regulations" concerning windows, doors, and fireplaces at The Nook. These were collected in a voluminous, handwritten copybook that the owner had left in the kitchen. She encouraged, nay commanded, us to read it and reread it. Otherwise, who knew what misfortune might befall us? The guidebook contained entries like this:

Bathroom: Extractor fan comes on when you switch on the light. If you have a shower in daylight, please put on the fan (pull switch over the hand basin) to remove moist air. Leave bathroom door slightly open for air flow.

Fly swat: Please take care not to break windows or do any damage if you are using this.

Mouse bait is hidden away in the cupboard under the stairs and in the airing cupboard. For the safety of pets and children, please keep these two cupboard doors shut. When the cottage is unoccupied in the winter months, sometimes small field mice creep in, but *don't worry,* you should not see any.

Green gate: Please check to make sure this is securely fastened. When you go out please shut gate by the car port. Cows wander down from the Common sometimes.

The notebook also contained entries under "bread" (where to get it), "ice cream" (locally made at Winstone's on Rodborough Common) and "toaster" ("Be careful; the bread pops up rather quickly, and do pull out and empty the crumb tray"). All told, the book featured more than a hundred distinct entries, all written in a patient, highly legible script. Many of them referred to children. ("*Balls:* Please do not let children play with these on the lawn. The asbestos roof on my garage and on the car port could so easily be damaged.") There were numerous admonishments against letting children play unsupervised; it was noteworthy that when the owner of The Nook, generally thought to be the author of *The Guide to the Nook* (though both John Fletcher and Francis Bacon may have been involved), warned guests about the mouse poison, she cited the potential danger to "pets" before the threat to "children." For instance, on the very same page that carried the entry:

> *Children:* Please do not let them play with balls in the garden or damage any property or play with my television set.

there was also a subentry that read:

> *Small children:* Please do not let them play upstairs unsupervised.

The handbook was rigorously cross-referenced, with sagacious dictums about the extraction unit and the handmade ice cream on Rodborough Common making several appearances. Some entries seemed like a bit of a stretch:

> *House:* Please take care of everything as if it were your own.

and

> *Defects:* Please mention any defects in equipment, etc., so that they can be put right.

but most did not.

My own children, eleven and eight at the time, loved to read the guidebook out loud. They particularly enjoyed the more extraneous comments such as:

> *Holidays:* are so important. Rest, refreshment, break with routine, change of scenery are all so necessary in the busy lives we all have to live. Please enjoy your holiday at The Nook.

They also tittered at the only entry appearing under the letter Y, which read:

> *You.* Never forget that this vacation is about you, you, you.

The implied subtext in this exhortation was the possibility that some guests might actually forget to enjoy their holidays if they did not avail themselves of the sage counsel promulgated in the book. The children were surprised that there was not a single entry under the letter O, whose page was left blank, perhaps in the expectation that the proprietress would one day add the words:

> *Odin.* Fierce warrior god worshipped by the Saxons who once ravaged this area.

They were also disappointed that there was no entry for the letters Q and X. It seemed shocking that a person who had gone to so much effort to include "*Umbrellas*" and "*Jigsaws* in cupboard by the fireplace. There may be some pieces missing" should have omitted "*Xylophone:* Where to get them repaired in Little Badminton" or "*Xerxes:* Myth that Stroud

may have been founded by the Persians in the fifth century
B.C." Even more puzzling was the omission, "*Queen Elizabeth:*
long-suffering mother-in-law of spoiled brat Princess Diana."

THE NOTEBOOK WAS A PERFECT SYMBOL OF EVERYTHING I
had come to love or, in some cases, accept about the English.
They were nutty as a fruitcake. They were nuttier than a fruitcake. No fruitcake known to man could compass their lunacy.
They invited you over to watch decrepit videotapes of less-
than-boffo morris dancing or award-winning window insula-
tion techniques. They scheduled lunch at the Old Ladies Tea
Shop, where the ancient tartars in question blew cigarette
smoke all over the sticky buns. They told you to take the first
left past Frogmarsh Lane, right where Frogmarsh Mill Cottage adjoined South Cottage, North Cottage, and The Cottage. But if you went up Bospin Lane past the Brambles, you
had gone too far; you had to redescend to Lagger Lane until
you saw Plum Tree Cottage and then go up the hill to The
Olde Mill. They intimated that, if time permitted, and the
kiddies promised to be *very good,* they might be able to
squeeze in a visit to the Frog & Forge for a repast of Spotted
Dick and farm-fresh faggots. They kept a straight face when
they told you these things, and expected you to do likewise.
But you could not. For you came from America, which had
fruited plains, not *fruity* ones.

I am not sure if English people are in fact more interesting
than Americans, but, because the country is so small, it has
encouraged the citizenry to retreat inside their heads and
cultivate a kind of good-natured insanity. Because there are so

many oddballs living in such a confined space on this microscopic island, your chances of running into them grow exponentially. And because eccentricity of one sort or another is revered, rather than frowned upon as it is in America, the zaniness never ceases. I once saw a sign in Stroud outside a maudlin, semidetached Victorian house whose owners had written:

IF YOU WANT TO KNOW WHO ASSASSINATED THE TREE
THAT IS NOW CHOPPED NEATLY IN TWO BETWEEN
OUR TWO HOMES, CONSULT THE RESIDENTS NEXT DOOR.

Americans would never do this. They would simply move or sue or fetch the shotgun. But they wouldn't post an arch, abusive sign outside their homes, and if they did resort to a written communiqué, it wouldn't be funny, much less correctly punctuated.

The English are masters of obsequious, slightly unhinged, self-referential signage. In Gloucester, I saw a plaque with the words:

THE RESIDENTS OF BRUNSWICK SQUARE AND THE
COMMITTEE OF THE BRUNSWICK SQUARE CENTRAL
LAWN ASSOCIATION HAVE NO OBJECTION TO
MEMBERS OF THE PUBLIC ENJOYING THE GARDEN.

One got the impression that the residents of Brunswick Square and the Committee of the Brunswick Square Central Lawn Association had actually convened an emergency meeting and taken a vote to see if anyone *did* in fact object to members of the public enjoying the garden, or if they were amenable to *most* members of the public enjoying the garden, but had a few reservations about this or that individual.

In the entirely generic men's room of the British Council on Portland Place, I spied a placard that read:

THESE TOILETS ARE INSPECTED AND SERVICED AT REGULAR
INTERVALS EVERY DAY. IF YOU HAVE ANY COMMENTS OR
SUGGESTIONS, OR IF THE STANDARDS OF THE FACILITY DO NOT
MEET YOUR EXPECTATIONS, THEN PLEASE CONTACT
THE FACILITIES GROUP HELP DESK AT EXT. 5000.

This sort of officious bureaucratic twaddle provided a prism through which to view the English national character. I particularly liked the part about the facilities that might not meet the visitor's expectations; it suggested that someone might one day phone the Facilities Group Help Desk at extension 5000 and complain that there were no Empire Era chandeliers or Tiepolo murals above the urinals, which was the very least one could expect. I suspected that an entire army of functionaries sat marshaling their resources at the Facilities Group Help Desk, poised to spring into action should anyone call and express their dismay about the condition of the ladies' toilets or the absence of any Jean-Antoine Houdon busts of Marcus Aurelius in the shockingly lugubrious stalls.

NO ONE WRITING A BOOK ABOUT GREAT BRITAIN CAN AVOID discussing both the food and Winston Churchill, which are not connected in any way. My attitude on the former is simple: The food used to be bad, but now it is good.

Twenty-five years ago, it was all but impossible to get a good meal in the provinces, but that is now no longer the case. On the other hand, the food inside British homes was always a delight; I defy anyone, anywhere, to find a better meal than my sister-in-law's Sunday roasts, consisting of succulent, juicy prime beef and Yorkshire puddings the size of the Caucasus. And my wife is a far better cook than any American I have ever met. (She did spend some time working in a French hotel as a girl, but that does not explain her premium trifles.) When Americans announce that they went to Britain and were disappointed by the food, they are merely regurgitating hoary old clichés that have long since lost all validity. This is a particularly annoying trait of Americans from small towns whose finest dining establishment is the Red Lobster.

My problem in Britain has never been the quality of the food, but its availability. Restaurants from Linton Gorge to Great Malvern impishly list cherry pie on their menus, but the last cherry pie seen in Britain was a wee *clafoutis* that Bonnie Prince Charlie brought over from Lyon in 1745 as a portent of things to come. When I visited Manchester, whose delightful cathedral contains a wooden Tudor Era choir that the Luftwaffe and the IRA somehow managed not to incinerate, there was no coffee in the swish hotel. *No coffee.* I have never been able to get served a meal anywhere in Wales on a Sunday, and in Randwick, a tiny hamlet that preens directly above the Stroud That Nobody Knows, the landlord never explained why he could not serve my brother-in-law so much as a ploughman's lunch, merely remarking, "It's a bit difficult." It *is* a bit difficult in Britain.

Things would have been a lot more difficult had Winston Churchill not put in an appearance. All Americans revere Churchill, who stood against the Huns at the gates of Ramsgate the way Pope Leo I once stood against the Huns at the gates of Rome. (I apologize if Germans with no blood on their hands object to the use of the pejorative term *Huns*, but after Auschwitz and Dachau, all bets are off.) Still, Americans with conservative leanings make an absolute fetish out of the man. Adroitly skirting the booze, the archaic imperialism, and the disaster at Gallipoli, American solons hope that by genuflecting at the great man's tomb and claiming him as their spiritual antecedent, some of his light will reflect back on them. In their minds, if *they* had been on hand when all the rough stuff was going on back in the late 1930s, they too would have had the courage to face down Hitler and make the world safe for democracy, or at least for Poland.

These are the same people who insist that had *they* been manning the Maginot Line in 1940, they would have spilled their life's blood into the Ardennes escarpment rather than succumb to the Aryan darkness. Then they take a commuter local home to suburban Pleasantville and meekly hand over their wallets to insolent teenagers with baseball hats cocked at funny angles. I know some of these pundits, scholars, and think tank drones personally. Churchillian, they are not. Nor are the politicians who reap the fruits of their intellectual labors. When the enemy aircraft appeared over London in 1940, Churchill stayed in London, dispatching Simcox to the wine cellar for more champagne, all the while smoking gargantuan stogies. When the enemy aircraft appeared over

Washington in 2001, the would-be Churchills ran away and hid like church mice, then reconvened on Capitol Hill later that evening to sing a fulsome rendition of "God Bless America" once the danger had passed. Never, in the course of human events, had so many owed so little to so few.

Retroactively aligning oneself with Winston Churchill is hardly an act of political courage; it is like puffing out your chest, casting down the gauntlet, and unequivocally declaring that you will defend Mozart's work to the death, as if revering Salieri were a viable alternative. This repellent admiration for the obviously great is the stock-in-trade of the shallow politician and the facile editorial-page writer; it is like rooting for the New York Yankees or Manchester United and then acting as if some risk were involved. There is also something industriously stupid about the perpetual evocation of the Munich specter: Not every confrontation with every foreign tyrant is tantamount to staring down the Thousand-Year Reich. Churchill, who personally despised many of those who sat on his side of the aisle in Parliament, would be appalled by the sight of all these twenty-first-century wonks and wankers evoking his memory. Winston Churchill had standards.

I possess two distinct sets of feelings about Churchill. On the one hand, I am enormously grateful to him for saving the civilized world from the marauding Hun, as no one else alive at the time seemed terribly interested in the job. But I am also in his eternal debt because of his magnificent pen. Some people find it inappropriate that Churchill won the 1953 Nobel Prize for Literature; were there no Senegalese raconteurs or Bulgarian folklorists in the running that year? To these braying asses, I suggest that they read *A History of the English-Speaking Peo-*

ples. Composed in an admittedly hyperbolic prose that has long since gone out of fashion, Churchill's four-volume masterpiece is a clear and enthusiastic statement of the equally unfashionable idea that some civilizations are better than other ones, that some civilizations are no good at all, and that human beings, not economic forces, shape all of human history. He would know. Some seventeen hundred pages in length, *A History of the English-Speaking Peoples* is a ripping yarn, filled with the sort of pageantry and color that professional historians abhor. Typical is Churchill's description of Richard the Lion-Hearted's death in 1199; felled by an archer while besieging a Norman fortress during one of his typically hare-brained continental excursions, Richard insisted that the man responsible for his death be spared, as he was only performing a soldier's duty. The king's adherents vowed to do his bidding. The chapter's final paragraph contains a single sentence:

"The archer was flayed alive."

When *A History of the English-Speaking Peoples* was issued in an abridged version a few years ago, the anecdote about the archer was deleted.

The editor should be flayed alive.

Great Britain, of course, can lay claim to a long and noble tradition of eccentric popular historians, which America cannot. Edward Gibbon, Thomas Carlyle, and H. G. Wells were all in some way mad but made up for it by being brilliant and loads of fun. American popular historians are infrequently mad, rarely entertaining, and almost never brilliant. It's not in our genes; this is a literal society, not a literary one.

The greatest popular historian of recent vintage is A. J. P. Taylor, who died in 1990. I have read every one of his books, and view it as a tragedy that he is not better known in America, where hacks and bozos reign supreme. Taylor used to enrage his colleagues in the academy by setting forth extravagant theories like the notion that Adolf Hitler was just another land-grabbing German politician who happened to get in over his head. Though Hitler did end up becoming the Antichrist, Taylor believed this was a role he more or less drifted into; the Little Corporal never seriously thought the Allies would go to war over Poland when they had refused to go to war over Czechoslovakia. These are probably indefensible positions, but it was bliss to watch Taylor defend them. Taylor would also engage in lengthy digressions on alleged extraterrestrial intervention into battles fought on Belgian soil in 1914 (the Angels of Mons), which is just the sort of thing that academic historians despise. In describing Churchill in *English History, 1914–1945*, Taylor wrote:

Winston Spencer Churchill (1874–1965), grandson of duke of Marlborough and of American tycoon, Jerome: educated Harrow and Sandhurst; first lord of the admiralty, 1911–15; chancellor of the duchy of Lancaster, 1915; commanded a battalion in France, 1915–16; minister of munitions, 1917–19; secretary for war (and air), 1919–21; for colonies, 1921–2; supported Lloyd George on breakup of Coalition and defeated at Dundee, 1922; Conservative M.P. for Woodford, 1924–64; chancellor of the exchequer, 1924–9; left Conservative shadow cabinet and opposed concessions to India, 1931; supported Edward VIII at time of abdication, 1936; first lord of the admiralty and member of war cabinet, 1939–40; prime minister of National government and minister of defence, 1940–5; leader of Conservative party, 1940–55; Conservative prime minister, 1945, 1951–5; K.G., 1953; the saviour of his country.

In the halls of academe, this is just not done. It is simply not possible for a serious historian to include punch lines like that today; the academy would be in high dudgeon. The deconstructionists would sue. The fur would fly.

Paul Johnson is another great popular historian who invariably gets up the academics' noses. Like Taylor, he demonstrates a penchant for taking absurd positions. After he published his splendid book *A History of the American People*, several critics pointed out that he had misidentified Norman Rockwell, the Perry Como of pigment, as a genuinely great artist rather than the sappy clown he was. (He did the same thing in his more recent *Art: A New History*.) Worse, he had not written a single word about baseball. He who did not understand baseball, so the theory went, did not understand the American people. Of course, critics are always saying this sort of thing: He who does not understand kielbasa cannot understand the Poles, he who does not understand blandness cannot understand the Austrians, he who does not understand overpaying to eat duck kidneys stuffed with pig's testicles cannot understand the French.

But in this case, I think the critics may be onto something. When you sit down to write a history of the American people and you neglect to mention the national sport, it's a pretty good indication that you don't really understand what Americans *are*, only what they *do*. As W. Somerset Maugham once expressed it:

> It is very difficult to know people and I don't think anyone can ever really know any but one's countrymen. . . . You can only know them if you are them.

I mention this by way of apologizing for the things I have not discussed at length in this book. I have nothing to say about cricket and almost nothing to say about the royal family, other than that neither seems to be particularly exciting. Hundreds of years ago, the English people, for reasons only they can understand, invited laconic, emotionally distant Teutons to be their titular rulers. The interlopers, who did not seem to like the English, invariably raised stupid, vulgar children who liked them even less. As far back as the time of George IV, the British population was riveted by the exploits of the tactless Prince of Wales and his slutty wife, Caroline. As far back as the time of Edward II and Isabella, the nation was enthralled by rumors of officially condoned murder involving members of the royal family. Some things never change.

Many, many years ago, the template for the royal family was established: The king or queen was either dull or insane; the children, some of whom dabbled in architecture or spoke a few words of Welsh, were invariably thick as two planks. It is hard to see how anything has changed over the centuries; the British people, for whatever the reason, seem to like having the royals around. But I don't tell people in other societies how to run their countries. That's George Bush's job. In the end I accept my wife's verdict—borne out by poll after poll of the British public—on the matter: Tourism is one of Britain's vital industries, and the royals are good for tourism. Obviously, some royals are better than others.

In one of his books, Taylor remarked that of all the kings and queens since William of Orange, only one or two seemed to possess more than average intelligence. There seems little reason to doubt this assessment, certainly not today. The English have always gone back and forth between hard taskmasters (Henry VIII, Oliver Cromwell), irresponsible fops (Edward II, Charles II), and outright lunatics (Henry VI, George III), but mostly they fancy boneheads. The royals were invented eons ago because television did not yet exist. They were always primarily entertainers rather than leaders. Richard the Lion-Hearted was a knucklehead who only came home to England long enough to collect enough money so he could leave again. King John was a ne'er-do-well of the worst sort. Edward II was a party animal, as was Charles II. Henry V was a playboy who liked to fight; Edward VII a playboy who liked to play. Henry VI was mad as a hatter, George III mad as a dozen hatters. Richard III was a sociopathic hunchback, but, as previously noted, a very fine dancer. Henry VIII was a psychopathic madman. Queen Mary was a madwoman. William of Orange was a misanthrope and Anglophobe. Edward VIII was a Nazi sympathizer who gave up his crown for the love of a Baltimore swinger. The fact that the swinger in question was a divorcée was bad, the fact that she was American was skating close to the edge, but the fact that she hailed from Crabcake Corners was unforgivable. The current occupant of the throne, Elizabeth II, has presided with great aplomb and dignity over the gradual but inevitable disintegration of the British Empire. Neither flashy nor communicative, this paragon of bourgeois taste and home-spun attire seems like a very nice old lady who has had the misfortune to be hemmed in by a self-replicating battalion of ding-dongs.

Americans cannot understand the royal family, but they certainly do not want to see it go. If the survival of the British royalty were ever seriously threatened, both the Americans and the Japanese would intervene, possibly with nuclear weapons. I personally love Philip's outrageous off-the-cuff comments, such as the time he asked Maori spear wielders: "Do you still throw those things at each other?" *Smashing material, Phil.* And there will always be a place in my heart for Princess Di, who once appeared on the cover of *People* wearing a bright green Philadelphia Eagles jacket. The doomed princess perhaps did not know that the Eagles had not won anything since 1960. But then again, neither has the House of Windsor.

The truth is, every country needs a few things that it can market really well. The Brits market romance. No one goes to Great Britain because of anything that happened in recent memory; it is a repository of ancient dreams. How people can live inside this sort of society mystifies me. There you are trying to have a normal, twenty-first-century life debugging your software or devising a marketing plan for solar-paneled parking meters and suddenly eighteen busloads of Japanese tourists whiz by, looking for Mr. Gradgrind's house, Silas Marner's thatched cottage, or Percival Wren's grave. It must be exasperating.

WHEN I FIRST VISITED ENGLAND IN MARCH 1976, I ENTERED through the port in Southampton. Asked by the immigration clerk how long I planned to stay, I responded, "Hopefully, forever." He informed me that this would not be possible. This has been a source of at least partial regret ever since. All of us wish that we had nine lives, and if I had nine of them, I would give one to Britain. No, two. Perhaps as many as six. It is inexhaustible. It is enthralling. It is, in its own, middle-class, higgedly-piggedly way, the most exotic society the planet has ever known. It is the kind of country that when you arrive somewhere you had not previously thought of visiting (Cornwall, Primrose Hill, Brixton, Clapham Common, Inverness), it seems as if you have finally fulfilled a lifelong dream.

Two days before the Queen Mother's funeral, I returned to Brimscombe to ask the dotty proprietor of The Nook if I could photocopy her household guide. The guide was spanking new; the previous one had fallen to pieces, so she had taken pen in hand and composed an entirely new version. Certain updates had been added; other entries had inexplicably been deleted. Ominously, there was no longer a specific mention of *"Cows: Keep the Gate closed, as they sometimes come down from the Common."* I feared that the cows, like Grendel, had met a grisly fate.

When I set out for The Field House, it was clearly my intention to gather comic material for my book. But then the spry old codger invited me into her house and we sat in front of the telly, drinking tea, nibbling bickies, conversing about what the Queen Mother meant to England. Her eyes teared up; her England was no more. I was touched and, quite frankly, I was jealous. I would love to live in a country where the entire society mourned the passing of a national icon, rather than getting all worked up about the untimely demise of John Ritter. I would also love to live in a country where men could be as spontaneously silly as Monty Python, Benny Hill, and the cast of *The Mikado*. But it is not in us; recent American comedy is rehearsed, calculating, cruel, and joyless; the closest we get to unpremeditated silliness is Jim Carrey, who is Canadian. When Michael Palin and Terry Jones get dressed up in women's clothes, it's sidesplitting. When Robin Williams does it, it's creepy.

For similar reasons, I would love to live in a country where an old woman would write a cottage handbook with entries like:

Fur Collector in electric kettle. Please do not throw this way.

And then, when the notebook got all torn and tattered, she would buy a new one and write them out all over again. But Americans don't do things like that; they are too busy watching *Survivor* or devising schemes enabling their oafish progeny to infiltrate outstanding private schools. So when I reprint her madcap entries here, I do so not in a spirit of ridicule, but in a spirit of homage.

I have always believed that the seasoned tourist should never try to exhaust a nation's resources, but should always leave something for his next visit. On my trip to Britain, I finally got to see Penzance, York, Liverpool, Edinburgh, Manchester, Glasgow, Leeds, Nottingham, and Durham, all of which had been casualties of early visits to Aunty Margaret's. I also visited Hadrian's Wall and Tintagel. But I deliberately left out North Wales, the Scottish Highlands, the Shetlands, and the Isle of Skye, as well as the Lake District, because I wanted delicious venues to come back to. I went to Margate, but not Blackpool; I visited Portsmouth, where Francis Drake sailed from, but left out Hastings, where Caesar landed. I made it to the moors, but skipped the dales and the fens, as the moors are more interesting than the dales, and the fens seem too much like New Jersey. I visited the oldest cathedral in Britain, and the largest, but skipped the second tiniest because the people in Carlisle annoyed me. I doubt that they care.

This time around, I had no fixed departure date and decided to stay in Britain until I had completely run out of gas. For six weeks, I crisscrossed the country with inexhaustible resolve and energy, like Nelson pursuing the French fleet in 1805. (He did not set foot on dry land for two solid years, or so the story goes.) Some of my questions about this enigmatic society were never answered. I never found out why snooker tables are so big in a country that is so small. I never found out why my wife continues to drink loose tea after nearly everyone else her age has stopped, or whether it is true that Twinings has recently changed the formula for its legendary English Breakfast variety. I never found out who started the tradition of drinking Beaujolais on the sidelines at the Barnstable Rugby Club's Saturday matches, nor how the club's management expects the fans to follow the game's progress if the scorekeeper keeps leaving his tiles at home. I never learned what nautical conditions caused the tidal wave known as "the Bore" on the Severn, nor why the British people adore the sappy Bing Crosby vehicle *The Bells of St. Mary's*. I never got a satisfactory answer as to why the famous painting of Lawrence of Arabia was no longer hanging in the Tate

Britain or when the Serpentine stopped putting on good shows. It was not my good fortune to learn why John Hanning Speke killed himself on the eve of his greatest triumph, or what the widow of his deadly rival Richard Burton was thinking of when she burned his translation of the *Kama Sutra* the night of his death. To this day I have no idea how the legends of Saint George or P. G. Wodehouse got started. Nor did I ever learn the origin of the term *crikey,* but mindful of the dictum that one should never, ever use another nation's slang, I'm buggered if I'm going to use it now.

That is not all. I never found out why there was a dreadful painting of a voluptuous woman demurely attired in evening gown and halo in the church of St. Martin-within-Ludgate, but I had no trouble believing that this bizarre portrait of Saint Agnes—who got her breasts sliced off by the Romans in the second century—probably didn't go down that well with the congregation when it was first hung in the 1930s. I never found out whose idea it was to position the public toilets in Stroud right across the street from the Health Food Shop, nor why the public toilets in Kensington cost twenty pence, while the public toilets in the department stores in Brixton cost fifty pence. (It seemed to me that a country so obsessed with plumbing should have a uniform lavatory pricing code.) Finally, I never found out why the English invited uncongenial Dutchmen to run the country in 1688, then replaced them with even less affable Germans. The English have spent most of their history keeping the French out, but have gleefully invited other, equally reprehensible ethnic groups in. They must *really* hate the French.

— — —

MY TANK FINALLY RAN EMPTY DURING A VISIT TO YET ANOTHER
astonishing church built by Christopher Wren. My wife had
insisted that I attend the Sunday morning parade of the
Chelsea Pensioners, ancient warriors dressed to the nines in
bright red coats and silky black pants. But when I reported for
the review that day, Maggie Thatcher turned up as well,
attending her regular Sunday morning service in the chapel,
despite a recent stroke. Win, lose, or draw, Thatcher is an
iconic figure in British history, a tough woman among soft
men, and the fact that you could merely drift into a Sunday
morning church service and chant ancestral hymns along
with her was thrilling. (My wife once bumped into Hillary
Clinton at a snooty movie theater in Pleasantville, New York,
five miles from our home, but the effect was not the same:
Clinton is a Medici, Thatcher a full-blooded Borgia.) On the
other hand, Margaret Thatcher is the kind of person who
sucks all the air out of the room. After spending less than an
hour in her presence, I wandered over to Hyde Park,
stretched out on a bench, and took a badly needed two-hour
nap. Thatcher's effect was that fatiguing.

It was time to pack.

Only one item of unfinished business remained. A few
days later, I was desperately trying to get into Westminster
Cathedral to see the tomb of Ben Jonson for no good reason,
only to find that it was closed due to Commonwealth Day. A
bobby told me that the queen would be putting in an appearance around one in the afternoon, adding, "You Americans go

in for that sort of thing." We do, we do. I rushed back to my apartment near Victoria Station, showered, shaved, then grabbed a cab back to the abbey. The royals were already arriving, but the cabbie inexplicably dropped me off right at the front door scant seconds before Prince Charles arrived. The crowd waited with bated breath as I emerged from the taxi, doubtless expecting the Viscount of Mangotsfield. They were sadly disappointed. A bobby merely shook his head as I emerged from the taxi and waved me into the crowd, but no one tried riddling my body with high-powered rifles the way they would have had I pulled a similar stunt in Washington, D.C., when Dick Cheney or some equally mythical American politician was expected.

Shortly thereafter, the queen arrived, looking the way she always does. I stood not forty yards away and clicked a very nice photo of her signature handbag. Afterward I phoned my wife to tell her of my experience. When I returned home, my children reported that Francesca, slightly miffed, as she had never seen the queen up close and personal, had nevertheless gone out and bought flowers and "treats" to celebrate my good fortune. "Your father went to London to see the queen, and your father went to London and did see the queen," she told them. "Now, finish your Weetabix."

These trophies bagged, I knew it was time to go home. I'd had a smashing time of it; I honestly believe that my long hegira in Britain may have saved my life, as I was getting awfully tired of writing about America. Yet to this day, I do not believe that I am an Anglophile. The Anglophile wishes he were someone else, but I do not; just because I admire Mahatma Gandhi doesn't mean I want to be a short, bald, pacifist vegetarian. I am more than happy to be a tall, brooding Irish-American, and happy to live in a century where it is possible to marry an Englishwoman without ceaselessly having the Curse of Cromwell called down upon me by pseudo-Celtic IRA buffs from Totowa, New Jersey, who think that getting tanked up on Guinness and humming "The Minstrel Boy" on Saint Patrick's Day makes them the spiritual heirs of Michael Collins and Wolfe Tone. Besides, my wife is part Irish. I love Great Britain, but I will always be an outsider, an observer, a guest, and in some sense a tourist.

And yet, there is a personal Albion that belongs to me that no English citizen born in more recent times can ever know. I remember Stonehenge before the fence got put up around it, when you could simply drive up in the middle of the night and stand speechless before the mysterious monoliths. I remember the miners' strikes that caused Edward Heath's government to collapse. I remember Edward Heath. I even remember miners. I remember that Carmella's Place in Nailsworth used to be called Tubby's, and that the plumbing didn't work under that name either. I remember stone pubs in Paganhill that were so frigid you had to already be drunk just to stay warm enough to take off your gloves and pay for your next drink so you could get drunker. I remember a pub in Dursley with a ceiling so low that my dart once deflected off the roof into the bull's-eye, much to my brother-in-law's distress. I remember another freezing pub in Paganhill where my brother-in-law and I got doused in ice cold water by a drunken prankster who claimed to be aiming at somebody else, but Tony insisted on finishing our game of cribbage with the soaking cards because he had four fives and a queen with two kings in the box and wasn't likely to get another hand like that for the rest of his life. I remember another pub in Cheltenham that was too tiny to have a bar; you walked up to a kind of ticket booth to order your drinks. I remember . . . well, let's just say I remember a lot of pubs.

Much of the Britain that I love has disappeared. Edwardian pubs have been torn apart and remodeled to look Tudor; even in the dainty Cotswolds people rarely say things like "Excuse me, old cock; could I borrow that stool?" anymore. But enough of the old Britain remains. Anaïs Nin once wrote that everyone who comes to Paris regrets that the Paris he knew as a youth no longer exists. But she sagely observed that each generation discovers a new Paris. So it is with Britain. Everyone who comes to England fashions England to his liking. England is happy to accommodate.

WHEN MOST AMERICANS TRAVEL THEY ARE LOOKING FOR A sunny locale that can amuse them. I, on the other hand, am seeking an entire society. Once, while filming the final scene in my preposterously unsuccessful Channel 4 film *My Fair Hugh,* the director asked why I had such a beatific expression on my face. I told him that I was an American standing in a fog-swept London street with double-decker buses whipping past and bobbies marching up the alleyway, and that this was the American Dream. There isn't anything in the world better than riding a London double-decker bus. There isn't a more beautiful place in the world than the Embankment at sunset. There is nothing in the world more stirring than the Houses of Parliament illuminated at midnight, with the daunting visage of Oliver Cromwell staring down at you, brooding, "Cross me at your peril." (If Hitler had only seen the statue, he could have saved himself an awful lot of *sturm, drang, angst,* and *todt,* and would have picked a less resilient race to schedule a *götterdämmerung* with. Of course, he could have also learned this by standing in a steady drizzle with the season ticket holders at any Leyton Orient match.) I have often said that if I had to pick a city to live in the rest of my life it would be Paris, but if I had to pick a city in which to spend the last day of my life it would be London. One chilly evening, I called a friend in New York to gloat that I was standing in the shadow of Nelson's statue in front of the National Gallery right beside St. Martin-in-the-Fields as Big Ben struck midnight, and he had the misfortune to be elsewhere. You cannot put a price on these things, and if you did, it would not be nearly high enough.

I LEFT LONDON FOR NEW YORK THE DAY AFTER THE QUEEN Mother's funeral. Hundreds of thousands of ordinary people lined the streets. The service was broadcast over enormous loudspeakers lining St. James's Park; the silence was breathtakingly visceral. People were not afraid to weep openly, even if they considered the Queen Mother's Depression Era politics repugnant, her attitude toward the Germans in the prewar years discreetly airbrushed. After the funeral, the queen herself motored past; it was the second time I had seen her in the past month. She had just lost a sister, now her mother. She was having a tough time of it. At the very end of the service, the Grenadier Guards, the Highlanders, and all the rest marched past in their amazing, resplendent, and very strange costumes. There were kilts, bagpipes, massive furry hats, battered tiger skins ringing their torsos. The British may have lost their empire, but they still know how to put on an imperial show. The ancient pipes filled the air with the tunes that had petrified enemies from Bunker Hill to Bengal. The pipers sported the very stiffest of upper lips. I did not really want this to end; I did not want to go home; I did not want to be anywhere but Britain. Maybe next year I would forgo London for Rome. Maybe not.

As the last of the pipers disappeared toward their garrison near Buckingham Palace, and I gazed over the sea of teary-eyed Brits, I felt the same way I did whenever I heard Beethoven's Ninth Symphony, that it was hard to believe I had been lucky enough to live in the same solar sytem as such a remarkable human being. The English inspired a similar sense of affection and awe. They were, by turns, mad, hilarious, exasperating, unpredictable, peculiar, courageous, thrilling. The Brits were the very best mankind had to offer; if the planet was ever to host a more fascinating race, then the rest of us were in for a real treat. By taking my name, my wife had conferred on me perhaps the greatest gift an American can receive: the keys to the Kingdom by the Sea. Standing in the park as the drone of the bagpipes receded into the distance, I was reassured by the thought that there would always be Highlanders, there would always be Grenadier Guards, there would always be the queen, there would always be an England.

The alternative was simply not acceptable.

ACKNOWLEDGMENTS

The author wishes to leave no one unthanked.
Thanks to everyone.